ESL
428.34 ROT
Roth, Eric Hermann, 1961–
Compelling American
conversations : teacher
edition : with commentary, sup

18.95

COMPELLING AMERICAN CONVERSATIONS:
TEACHER EDITION

WITH COMMENTARY, SUPPLEMENTAL EXERCISES,
and REPRODUCIBLE SPEAKING ACIVITIES

Authors
Eric H. Roth
Mark Treston
Robert Glynn

Editors
Toni Aberson

NO LONGER THE PROPERTY
LONGMONT PUBLIC LIBRARY

CHIMAYO
PRESS

Copyright © 2015 by Eric H. Roth.
All rights reserved.

Roth, Eric Hermann, 1961–
Compelling American Conversation – Teacher's Edition: Questions & Quotations for
Intermediate American English Language Learners / written, compiled, and edited by
Robert Glynn, Eric H. Roth and Mark Treston; with Toni Aberson
p. cm.
Includes bibliographical references.

ISBN-13: 978-1512226751
ISBN-10: 1512226750   (Teacher Edition)

LCCN:2012930056
ISBN: 978-0-9826178-9-2   (Student Edition)
ISBN: 978-0-9847985-0-6 (e-book)
ISBN: 978-1468158366 (Create Space)

1. English language—Conversation and phrase books.
2. English language—Textbooks for foreign speakers.
3. Americanisms.
4. Quotations, American.
I. Aberson,Toni. II. Bogotch, Hal. III. Title.

Photographs by Dollar Photo Club (dollarphotoclub.com)
Cover Image from iStockphoto.com

Student Edition cover and book design by Stacey Aaronson;
Teacher Edition cover and book design by Andrea Schmidt

To order additional copies, share comments, ask questions, or contribute quotations,
please visit:
www.compellingconversations.com, or e-mail: eric@compellingconversations.com.

Chimayo Press
3766 Redwood Avenue
Los Angeles, California 90066-3506
United States of America
+1.310.390.0131
1-855-ESL-Book (toll free)
1-855-375-2665

www.CompellingConversations.com
www.ChimayoPress.com

LONGMONT PUBLIC LIBRARY
LONGMONT, COLORADO

Dedicated to

Dani Herbert Joseph Roth

(1937–1997)

An American by choice, he found safety, liberty, and prosperity in the United States.
He created compelling conversations, in six different languages, and left vivid memories.
This book attempts to capture some of his curiosity, generosity, and philosophy.

❝ America needs new immigrants to love and cherish it.”

—Eric Hoffer (1902–1983), *American writer and longshoreman*

❝ You are never strong enough that you don't need help.”

—César Chávez (1927–1993), *American civil rights leader*

❝ Our lives begin to end the day we become silent about things that matter.”

—Dr. Martin Luther King, Jr. (1929-1968), *American civil rights leader*

❝ We hold the power, and bear the responsibility. We shall nobly save,
or meanly lose, the last best hope of earth.”

—President Abraham Lincoln (1809-1865), *16th President of the United States*

TABLE OF CONTENTS

HOW THIS BOOK WORKS   i-x

Chapter One: Opening Moves   1

Chapter Two: Going Beyond Hello   10

Chapter Three: Making and Breaking Habits   15

Chapter Four: Studying English   22

Chapter Five: Being Yourself   29

Chapter Six: Choosing and Keeping Friends   33

Chapter Seven: Playing and Watching Sports   38

Chapter Eight: Talking about American TV   45

Chapter Nine: Celebrating American Holidays   54

Chapter Ten: Being Stylish   61

Chapter Eleven: Handling Stress   66

Chapter Twelve: Practicing Interviews   71

Chapter Thirteen: Valuing Money   75

Chapter Fourteen: Exploring Cities   82

Chapter Fifteen: Photographs   87

APPENDIX

Reproducible Exercises   92

Quotes and Proverbs Worksheets   95

Adding Your Voice to Class Discussions   97

Hedging Language   99

Tips to Becoming More Active
in Classroom Discussions   102

Some Media Suggestions   104

PLUS: Search & Share Compilations

INTRODUCTION
• •

How do we get our intermediate English language learners to speak more in our classes? How can we help prepare American residents by choice develop the conversational skills to become future American citizens? What quotations and proverbs help explain diverse American perspectives and attitudes on some common conversation topics?

These questions inspired Compelling American Conversations: Questions and Quotations for Intermediate American English Language Learners. Since 2012, the versatile speaking skills textbook has found its way into several English as a Second Language and English language development classrooms. The book also gained some fans, including two friends and experienced ESL teachers, Mark Treston and Robert Glynn, in Los Angeles.

We met and discussed the many different ways, and many different teaching environments, that the English teachers use the book. Mark, Robert, and I created this reproducible English teacher's guide out of those wide-ranging, long conversations.

This book provides teaching notes, brief comments, and supplemental exercises for Compelling American Conversations based on ESL classroom experiences and reflections. The authors' skill, expertise, and passion for teaching English can be discerned in their many practical classroom tips. Even though I co-authored the original book, I also learned from their insightful teaching suggestions. Perhaps you will too.

Following the suggestion of many adult education and community college instructors, this Teacher Edition allows teachers to make classroom copies of pages from the Search & Share pages of the original book.

Like many other experienced English teachers, I often browse through teaching guides for ESL & ELT textbooks. Therefore, this particular Teacher Edition has been written so the materials can be read – and perhaps enjoyed - both individually or consumed in a scaffold manner. The two dynamic teachers and authors have shared their perspectives in a more candid, less diplomatic manner than many more traditional textbook publishers. The result is an informative, street smart guide to deploying Compelling American Conversations in your English classroom.

Take a look, use what you find valuable, and share with students. It's time for you and your English students to create some new compelling American conversations.

Sincerely,
Eric H. Roth, *Co-author of Compelling American Conversations*

HOW TO USE THIS BOOK

* *

"Start with the end in mind." 🌿 Ancient Greek proverb

Words can often have multiple meanings, and the term "intermediate English language learner" is no exception. Compelling American Conversations was written with this recognition to offer various ways of helping English students develop and deepen their conversation skills. Compelling American Conversations (CAC), an exceptionally flexible ESL textbook, makes adding speaking skills relatively easy in a wide range of classroom environments. Some English teachers work on semester schedule, some teach on briefer trimester schedules, and some English instructors lead summer classes for a single month. This Reproducible English Teacher's Guide to Compelling American Conversations provides teaching tips, brief comments, and supplemental exercises so you can help teach speaking skills in a relaxed, confident manner.

This intermediate American English textbook will help you feel more comfortable in English. It will also help you become more fluent in English – and become whom you want to be in the United States.

How Do You Use Compelling American Conversations in Multilevel Classes?

CAC also provides an invaluable resource for teachers in the common situation of teaching multi-level adult classes with ongoing enrollment. ESL teachers with multi-level classes must plans lessons that address the needs of the new students constantly entering the class without repeating material studied weeks or months ago by longtime students already in the class. CAC provides an ideal remedy for this situation, as topics, vocabulary and skills can be revisited without repeating the exact same material.

For example, a teacher who is teaching job interview skills to her students might cover CAC pages 80-81 in February. By the following May, this same teacher has 12 new students in her class, as well as 15 of the students from February. She needs to cover job interview skills again to meet the objectives in her course outline, but she doesn't want to repeat the exact same material that 15 of her students already covered in February. What can the teacher do?

CAC has the solution. If the teacher covered CAC pages 80-81 in February, now, in May, she can review the vocabulary on page 81, and continue on to material that will be new for all students on pages 82-86. Teachers of multi-level classes can keep these options in mind when using CAC, maintaining material in reserve for lessons in the weeks and months ahead.

Lessons can also be adapted to the needs of your individual students and instructional schedule. Of particular value to multi-level groups is the capacity to initiate a topic in one chapter, and then return to the same topic weeks or months later for review, or to introduce the topic to a new group of students, or to a group which includes former students.

These activities will help you to:

- Ask clear, simple questions

- Listen to each other

- Respond to questions

- Use common conversation starters

- Learn how to continue conversations on many current and timeless topics

- Discover and use new vocabulary words

- Memorize some American saying and some old proverbs

- Discuss ideas by studying classical and modern quotations

- Express your opinions and support your statements

- Find and share Internet resources about living in the United States

- Speak English with greater confidence

- Enjoy learning about your classmates and yourself

"Practice makes perfect," goes an old proverb. So we will practice speaking English in every class. We will also learn more by asking questions. And we will learn by doing.

Developing conversation skills remains the focus of this book. Therefore, each chapter includes a series of conversation questions. Some questions will be direct; some indirect. The questions usually move from simple to more abstract. Students will also be given many opportunities to ask additional questions in order to both learn and use new vocabulary words.

EXPANDING VOCABULARY

While many textbooks introduce vocabulary lists first, we have chosen to let students first create a conversation and learn a bit by doing. Students can confirm or learn the meanings of words in this vocabulary exercise.

ASKING QUESTIONS

Students, even at the advanced levels, often find the grammar of asking questions difficult. Therefore, CAC includes a section for students to practice writing questions in each chapter. You can have students ask each other these original questions for additional conversation practice.

You can circle around the room and check students' question for grammatical accuracy too. We find that many of our ESL students appreciate this written feedback, especially in an oral skills class where they might not expect to receive it. Multi-skills classroom teachers can also assign this activity for homework.

The section **"The Conversation Continues"** in each chapter is ideally suited to continuing, expanding and deepening conversations with and between your students. This section can also be held in reserve by the teacher and returned to in a later lesson for review and to give the students additional conversation practice.

IDIOM EXERCISES

These exercises are designed to be scaled up for more advanced students or simplified for students who are not quite ready for the objectives. Feel free to adapt exercises to the needs of your students.

Note: *American English abounds with wonderful idioms. In this Teacher's Guide, you will periodically see a parenthetical (explain idiom) placed after particular idioms that occur in the text. What this bold-face indicator signifies is that when using this expansion or extension activity with students, you can/should explain this particular idiom or expression to them so that they understand what it means and how it is used.*

The Brave and the Bold

This section of the Teacher's Guide is designed for teachers who are more adventurous and open to exploration. The suggestions may not work with all teachers and classroom environments, as some topics may be too sensitive or controversial for some classroom settings. However, with the proper teacher guidance and classroom environment, these activities can prove fascinating and productive.

CAUTION: This section identifies areas with additional issues that mandate instructor awareness. Some topics may provoke an emotional response in certain students. None of these issues should be reason to avoid these topics entirely, as the students comprise a vast spectrum of human beings, and their responses often cannot be predicted. For example, one student might spontaneously burst into tears during a lesson on family. You might discover this is because she misses her family and her emotional reaction changes the class atmosphere. This possibility does not mean that you should never do a lesson on family because someone might start crying.

If you allowed yourself to be constricted by such issues, you could never teach a lesson on anything, as any topic can be problematic in some way to some student somewhere. For example, Chapter 15, on photographs, could potentially be offensive to students from religious groups that prohibit photography or tribal societies that believe that the taking of photographs steals the soul of the person. Balance, as ever, remains essential.

It is much better and more practical to use your own judgment as well as school and community standards. For example, in the above situation, it is best to be careful about letting the loudest, most narrow-minded students set the standards for everybody else. You can explain that in the United States (as well as virtually everywhere else), most people enjoy photography and enjoy taking, seeing, and sharing pictures. This widespread appreciation enjoyment of photography can be seen by the inclusion of cameras on smart phones and lack of prohibitions on photography in public. If these students continue to object, keep in mind that adult schools are voluntary and they are free to not participate. You can also choose to change the topic to prevent any uncomfortable subject. It's your call.

We would like to note however that universal education remains a great way to change lives and improve our world. Even the very presence of any women in your classroom is offensive to some Islamic zealots. Clearly, unlike some violent religious bigots in Afghanistan, Pakistan and Nigeria, we believe everyone has a right to a quality education – including girls and women too often historically excluded.

Fun with Famous Folks

This activity can be used with every chapter. Each chapter of CAC contains ten quotations from a wide variety of well-known writers, statesmen, politicians, artists, architects, musicians, athletes, thinkers and other luminaries. It is likely that many of these names will be unfamiliar to many or even most of your students, depending on their age and country of origin. A fun activity that can be done with every chapter is to assign students to research the lives and work of particular personages from each chapter. You can also pick which figures to assign to which student or group of students.

Alternately, you can let the students gravitate towards and select the people they are most curious to learn about. These students can then research the lives of their subjects at the library or on the internet, and give a presentation in class about what they found, and who the individual people are.

Make sure your students do not simply copy chunks of information off the internet from Wikipedia and other sources. While your students can and should consult these sources for information, they should be able to write and say the information in their own words, and understand what they are saying.

Connection, and Citizenship Connection

Before your students present their findings to the class, go over their material with them and make sure they are in firm command of their facts. This individualized feedback will help your students avoid embarrassment when fielding questions from their fellow students, as they will be able to answer with confidence.

Grammar Connection, Vocabulary Connection, Pronunciation

These sections highlight areas of lessons that can be coordinated with grammar, pronunciation and vocabulary topics that you may be covering in your class.

Steps to Success

The teachers' edition serves as a guide for educators who want to take those extra steps to insure successful learning outcomes for their students. In addition to specific, individual tips for teachers, we have added three new sections to deal with the most commonly asked questions, by both educators and students. This work is the culmination of the pooling of ideas and the sharing of experiences of an eclectic group of educators and administrators in the tightly-knit ESL community of Los Angeles. These educators come from both prestigious institutions and small private language schools and we have listened to and learned from them all. The end result is Compelling American Conversations: Teachers' Edition.

We've reviewed the general structure of the book. Now let's take a detailed look at each individual exercise in each of the book's 15 chapters.

How do you flip your English class? What speaking activities do you use to spark ESL discussions in small groups?

How do you create lively small group discussions in your English class? What homework do you find most likely to spark student-led conversations? Are you interested in flipping your ESL class so English language learners collect information outside of class and share the information inside the class?

One effective teaching technique we've often used is called "Search and Share". This communicative internet homework activity encourages - actually requires - English students to take an active role in their English classes. The ESL or EFL students find their own videos and newspaper articles that match their interests, summarize the material, and evaluate its quality. Search and Share also allows students to also share more of their personal interests with classmates in a safe, focused manner on chosen themes.

What is Search and Share?

Over the last six years, we have used Search and Share activities as homework in intermediate and advanced high school and university English classes. The popular activity can be used for supplemental speaking exercise or extended into an entire class. Because students often want to present compelling material, they will spend far time reviewing possible videos and articles than we would ever require for homework too – and they become far more familiar with the concepts too.

English students share the information they have collected (job interview advice, review of a favorite film, product information/review, a TED talk, restaurant review, local tourist destination, favorite charity/non-profit, etc). Then, students break into small groups of 3-5 students at a small table or a circle of chairs. Soon everyone presents their "research", and the other students proceed to ask at least one question each. Each round usually takes 15-20 minutes to finish a search and share in university classrooms.

Speaking Exercise Can Easily Be Repeated to Improve Speaking Skills

Teachers can also move students into new groupings, and take the communicative activity a few steps further. Students can present their "research" again, but this time they must include all the information that they were asked in the first round. So the second telling provides more details. It's also usually tighter. Once again, however, every student asks every presenter a question. This practice pushes shy students to ask questions, and gives all students practice in responding to questions in English.

In a 50-minute class, we usually only have time for two rounds. Yet in an 80-minute class we usually have time for three rounds and a class discussion. As a teacher, I circle around in different groups, ask questions, and take notes. I usually summarize some good mistakes at the end of class and ask students to post the links to their selected videos or articles on a class website so other students can easily access the recommended materials. Sometimes students will be asked to develop a PPT presentation and prepare a class presentation for the following class. Students consistently praise this assignment on their course evaluations – and students speak almost the entire class.

In our latest book, Compelling Conversations – Japan, you can also find Search and Share exercises at the end of each chapters While specially designed for English language learners in Japan, you can easily adapt and deploy the worksheets for EFL/ESL classrooms across the globe.

Eric H. Roth, *Co-author of Compelling American Conversations*

CEFR Correlations

The CEFR (Common European Framework of References) is a guideline used to describe achievements of learners of foreign languages. The English guideline has made substantial inroads into the ESL world with several books and lessons referencing the CEFR level in the book. The level code (A1, A2, B1, B2, C1, C2) provides students and teachers with a better understanding of what level the book should be used for. The teacher's edition guide draws from the CEFR manual as well as experienced teachers' own lesson plans for each chapter's learning objectives.The following chart demonstrates Compelling American Conversations suggested use:

Exams and Tests		Recommended use as a supplementary guide for speaking, pronunciation and listening	Recommended use of Compelling American Conversations as a textbook for communicative and written skills		
		B1 Low Intermediate	B2 Intermediate	C1 High Intermediate	C2 Advanced
TOEFL iBT	Reading	8	22	28	29
	Listening	13	21	26	
	Speaking	19	23	28	
Cambridge ESOL Cambridge ESOL	General English	PET	FCE	CAE	CPE
	BEC	Preliminary	Vantage	Higher	
	YLE				
Pearson Test of English	PTE General	2 Intermediate	3 Upper Inter.	4 Advanced	5 Proficient
	PTE Academic	43-58	59-75	76-84	
TOEIC L&R	Listening	275	400	490	
	Reading	275	385	(455)	
TOEIC S&W	Speaking	120	160	200	
	Writing	120	150	200	
IELTS		3.5-4.5	5.0-6.0	6.5-7.0	7.5-9.0
	Writing	17	21	28	
	Total	57-86	87-109	110-120	

Added Topics

Accent Reduction Skills

As educators who have travelled the world, we appreciate diversity. We do not necessarily endorse "American" or "British" accents. Dialects and accents are extensions of identity, an indicator of a person's background and experiences. They are a personal touch that invites the listener to open up a conversation, often revealing interesting information about the speaker. Nevertheless, we know that especially in the world of business it is imperative for our students to be clearly understood. Therefore, we have included tips and suggestions as to how to achieve clarity of expression, whether the student speaks English with an "American," "British," or even "Australian" or "South African" accent.

English for Specific Purposes

We have been asked, almost on a daily basis, to address an aspect of the English language that falls primarily under the umbrella of 'English for Specific Purposes.' As some of us have had experience writing guidebooks tailored for Business, Academic and Medical fields, we felt we were in a position to respond to the global demand by contributing our expertise. One of the most useful vocabulary building tools for intermediate and advanced students is the emphasis on the study of prefixes and suffixes. By teaching some basic prefixes and suffixes, students can grow their English vocabulary skills exponentially.

Language learners are more effective at recognizing patterns rather than memorization. Therefore, it can dramatically improve students' vocabulary knowledge by simply learning some basic rules about prefixes and suffixes. Any language learner fears words that seem to have many letters. Psychologically, they assume these are difficult words for a more advanced student with some academic background. However, we know that by simply knowing prefixes that mean no/not such as: un/il/ir/im/non can immediately help students recognize that they already know the root of the word and now know what happens when we add these prefixes. For example, many students already know the word filtered. By adding "un" in front of the word, it now means "not" filtered. In this teacher's edition we added this as an optional lesson for each chapter to further improve students' vocabulary.

Phrasal Verbs

One of the most frustrating aspects for students of English is Phrasal Verbs. Native speakers use them on a daily basis and without noticing how complex they are. While idioms come and go (think "it's raining cats and dogs" and "cloud nine") phrasal verbs are embedded in written English as well as in our daily conversations. Simply changing a verb, preposition or article immediately changes the meaning of the entire phrase or sentence. Our students need and are especially interested in achieving a better understanding of this particularly gnarly feature of English. For this reason we added commonly used phrasal verbs to each chapter with brief explanations.

In order to facilitate a more engaging classroom environment, we suggest that you arrange your class to a more conversation-based environment. We realize that some instructors move from room to room, however it makes a large difference to at least arrange the chairs so that students feel comfortable moving around making eye contact with one another as opposed to just speaking with the instructor.

Creating a Conversation-Friendly Classroom

Many classrooms today include chairs on rollers making both partner and small group work far easier. At University of Southern California, the language classrooms also include small tables where four students can comfortably sit together and talk. From our perspective, this simple seating arrangement seems almost ideal for small group discussion.

In more traditional classrooms, some teachers find arranging the chairs in a u-shape or circle will allow students to feel equal to one another and be able to address each other. This arrangement also improves student interactions by prompting shy students to speak and not hide behind other students or sitting in the back. Furthermore, it inhibits students from distractions such as electronic devices.

If you do have access to your own classroom, we recommend that you decorate the walls with visuals. Posters pictures, and maps create an engaging, dynamic learning environment.

Visuals are key when teaching a language as we all know, and nothing works better than having visuals to use immediately as opposed to looking it up somewhere. Put up calendars, maps, pictures, grammatical rules, funny and thought provoking sayings, quotes and proverbs and even old-school chalkboard where students can express themselves every morning (chalkboards have become popular in trendy cafes and restaurants). Try to have access to technology such as a smart board or at least a laptop and projector. While some feel videos such as TED talks audio such as the Moth Radio Hour are important, we still emphasize the physical over the virtual world.

Chapter One: Opening Moves

Learning Objectives

→ Students will able to have engage in an introductory conversation

→ Students will be able to ask for help, clarify what was being discussed and offer basic information about themselves

→ Students will be able to use write basic sentences using present and past tenses

→ Students will be able to enunciate their words more carefully

→ Students will be able to understand basic quotations and proverbs and use them in conversations

→ Students will be able to share their ideas and ask questions

→ Students will be able to search and share information from different media outlets

p. 1 Meeting Each Other

This popular icebreaker activity gets students talking on the first day of class. Pair students by random numbers, initials, lineup or whichever pairing technique works best for your class.

Keep the conversation going: Encourage the students to continue their conversations with their own questions. This conversational activity will also help you perform a needs assessment on your students in the first few days of the class by observing their proficiency in making spontaneous conversation.

Pronunciation Connection: Give examples of words in English that are commonly pronounced with different accents, even by native speakers: Tomato, a, the, etc. Also, remind students to be clear about differentiating verbs, nouns, gerunds and adjectives with similar words such as drive, driver, driving and driven. This clarification prevents unnecessary confusion in conversation. These distinctions are classically expressed as learning to "say what you mean, and mean what you say."

Grammar Connection: It would help students to note that quotation marks (" ") in writing differentiate what we are saying from what someone else is saying. Quotations remain crucial not only for writing skills but also for reading and even listening. This might be an opportune time to delve into the use of quotations and paraphrasing for more advanced students.

p. 3 Expanding Vocabulary

Review definitions with students, with oral reading and/or repetition. This can be done teacher to student(s), or between students, depending upon context and student proficiency.

For practice and comprehension checks, ask students to clarify the vocabulary:

- What is the difference between agree and argue?

- What is the difference between conversation and talking, or simply asking questions and making requests? (I.e. how much does this cost?)

- Explain and explore the role of conversation in English speaking culture, in such venues as the pub, the bar, the coffee house, the "water cooler" at the workplace, in a park or out in nature, at an auditorium, or on the street etc.

Also, emphasize the extra-social importance of conversation: getting along with co-workers at your job, or being able to speak clearly at an interview. Explain how in mainstream American culture, people who are not conversational at all can make others uncomfortable and even nervous. As noted below, other cultures can have very different attitudes towards moments of silence in conversations.

Conversation Idioms:

Caution: Use your judgment as a teacher as to which idioms and expressions are appropriate for your particular school, class and student population.

Water Cooler Conversation – Workers in offices and other worksites congregate and gossip when getting glasses of water at the water cooler, or cups of coffee in commons or kitchen. "Water cooler conversation" usually consists of talking about what was on TV programs, movies, sports, general chat, "small talk," *(explain idiom, see below)* and office gossip.

✳*Small talk* – make conversation about the weather, sports, family and other prosaic, every-day topics, usually to start a conversation, socialize with and get to know strangers, or acknowledge respect for and awareness of co-workers, relatives, and other people. NOTE: You can explain that Americans tend to feel uncomfortable and awkward with moments of silence. This feeling differs from some other cultures and language groups, such as Japan, where silent stretches in conversation are prized as moments of harmony. This difference is good to keep in mind, as sometimes people from other countries can perceive Americans as talking continuously, whether or not they have anything to say.

Chit Chat – Innocent small talk. It can become disruptive and distracting when it occurs during class.

Chat him/her/me/you/us up – Talk to an attractive person with the intention of getting to know him or her better and possibly getting a date. (Although this expression is from Britain, it is "catching on" (explain idiom) in the United States.

Back talk – A heated response, often to a parent or other authority figure, usually without listening or considering what the other person has to say.

Talk past each other – Arguing couples, co-workers and others who state their opinions without listening to what the other person has to say.

✓ "Caller Talk"

Sound Practice Minimal Pairs:

Ear, year fear, gear, near, beer, deer, jeer, peer, tear. Also compare them to sounds distinguishing the vowels such as:

Long e sound	Short e sound	Long I sound
Beer	Bear	Buyer
Deer/Dear	Dare	Dire
Hear	Hair	Hire
Peer	Pair	Spire

Ask students in groups or pairs to come up with similar words and sounds to emphasize the dramatic changes pronunciation makes in the meaning of words and sentences.

p. 3 Expanding Vocabulary

State opinions and ask the students if they agree or disagree.

- I think American cars are better than Japanese or German cars.
  Do you agree or disagree?

Alternate activity: Write one or several opinion statements on the board and have students decide if they agree or disagree, and explain why, in pairs or groups.

Present these statements for consideration:

- Money is the most important thing in life. Do you agree or disagree?
- Love is more important than money in life. Do you agree or disagree?

You can do one or more of these statements, individually or in combination, to elicit the thoughts and expressions of your students.

This is an opportunity to discuss fact versus opinion. For example, the statement "I think American cars are better than Japanese or German cars" versus "American car companies posted record profits for the months of July and August" or "Highway safety tests list American car companies at the top of their ratings" (followed by more specific sources).

Here are some other questions you can use for this activity:

- How many people have children?

- Do you encourage your children?

- How do you encourage your children?

- How do we encourage each other in class?

- How do I encourage the students as a teacher?

- How do teammates encourage each other in a sport?

- Do you feel encouraged today? Why or why not?

- What things require courage to do? (This is an opportunity to discuss courage, encourage and discourage).

p. 5 Paraphrasing Proverbs

Discuss the meanings of the various proverbs, and how these reveal differences among cultures. You can also note that some different proverbs carry the same meaning. Discuss different phrasing, such as "Chance favors the prepared mind" and "The smallest journey begins with a single step." It is also worth exploring American ideas about opinions. Because of our constitutionally-guaranteed idea of free speech, Americans have the expression, "Everyone is entitled to his own opinion." This common expression has produced some amusing variations, such as "Everyone's entitled to my opinion."

You can lead students to compare and contrast the subtle differences in quotations:

" Today is the first day of the rest of your life."

" Live each day as if it is your last, for one day you will be right."

" Time was invented so everything wouldn't happen at once."

" If you can't say something nice, don't say anything at all."

" Knowledge (wisdom) begins with realizing (understanding) what you don't know."

" You can't teach an old dog new tricks."/"You're never too old to learn."

" If opportunity knocks, make sure you get up and answer the door."

" Talk is cheap"/"Silence is golden."

" Money talks, baloney (nonsense) walks."

" You are your own worst enemy."/"People cause their own problems."

Expansion Activity:

Modify proverb and create a new saying! Choose the ideas expressed in the proverbs and quotations, and invent your own variations! If you have a good memory and want to build group rapport, you can later include their original proverbs and sayings through your subsequent classes. If you feel really adventurous, you can promise your students to propagate their proverbs through your subsequent classes.

It will help students to explain and explore the definitions and concepts of literal, metaphoric, figurative, figure of speech and expression. Students might otherwise be baffled by expressions that they might be trying to translate and interpret literally.

Many expressions use imagery to make their point and convey their idea. For example, "People who live in glass houses shouldn't throw stones." Should such people also avoid sleeping during daylight hours? However, this expression does not refer literally to people who live in houses that are constructed entirely from glass. Rather, it advises us to consider our own vulnerabilities and shortcomings before we criticize or attack other people.

Give examples of literal and figurative expressions, and have the students differentiate each one. "Whenever you point a finger, you have four other fingers pointing back at you."
Ask your students what they think this expression means. Is this saying a literal or figurative expression? You can actually suggest to your students that they point their index fingers, and have them decide if their other fingers are indeed pointing back at them or not.

Be sure to give the students credit for the proverbs they invent. Here are some examples of a proverb invented in and for the class led by Robert Glynn English class in Los Angeles:

- "The Great Wall of China started with a single brick."

- "The Eiffel Tower in Paris started with an idea."

p. 8 Search and Share

Almost everybody knows the concept of body language. However, students are unfamiliar with the phrase "body language." You might consider explaining the concept of "body language" for students who might not be familiar with it. You can test your own aptitude for non-verbal expression by acting out various adjectives for the students and let them guess which feeling you are trying to convey.

Once students have done this, you can explain how this is "body language." You can have students repeat this fun exercise throughout the class. This exercise a great opportunity to discuss body language in other cultures. This has always been a conversation starter and everyone can share their experiences despite conversational skills. In fact, you could mime different body languages (as long as they are acceptable of course) as an activity and elicit students to respond. If the class is diverse, have students go around the room and interview fellow students for body language that is used in their country/culture.

A variation on this activity is to have students watch television news in English for 5-10 minutes, then report back to the class on what the main news story was and what it said. This alternative allows students to practice listening to native English speakers outside the classroom environment, discussing subjects and events that are at least somewhat familiar.

p. 9 On your own

This section is practice for the students in observing non-verbal communication (body language) and how this observation enhances and reinforces verbal communication in English. Where you and your students can practice this depends on where you are teaching, a big city with hordes of commuters riding the subway every day, or a small town with groups of people congregating in the town square, or anywhere in between.

EXPANSION ACTIVITIES

Academic Vocabulary Expansion: Prefix/Suffix Study
Prefixes alluding to "Not"

Non, Mis, un, a, non

It might be a great opportunity to discuss the evolution of the English language and some of the interesting surprises of where words come from. Words such as "uncommon" and "inaudible were first used in Shakespeare's plays and have been used ever since. Shakespeare basically combined the prefixes "un" and "in" to words to simply mean "not." This could lead to discussions about how language is constantly changing and that even the new age of technology relies heavily on prefixes, suffixes, roots and stems (internet, microchip). This is also a great conversation starter for the use of technology or words that are universally used across different languages.

Here are just a sampling and feel free to give examples in sentences.

Non:

> *Nonnative speaker* – One who does not speak the native language.

> *Nonconformist* – One Who does not conform to the existing social system.

> *Nonviolent* – One who does not believe in using violence as a method

Mis:

> *Misunderstanding, miscommunication, misinterpret, misconstrue, misinform, misuse.*

Un:

> *Uncompromising, unconditional, unsuspecting, unbelievable.*

A:

> *Amoral, asexual, atheist, apolitical, apathy.*

Phrasal Verbs

Two verbs that are commonly used at phrasal verbs are "take" and "make." One could use several lessons just going over the intricacies of the use of these two verbs in an English conversation. Do not forget to mention that phrasal verbs such as make up and take out have several meanings and therefore are even more confusing for students. This is the reason why students must remember to listen and read for context as opposed to individual words. This will also assist them in getting better scores exams such as TOEFL and IELTS.

Take out, after, over, apart, in, up, back;
Make out, of, over, though

This is a good opportunity to show how phrasal verbs can be separated.

> *Example:* George took his girlfriend out for dinner in Little Italy to celebrate her birthday. Did you make it through exam week intact?

Take Out – To remove something from somewhere.

> (a) Johnny, could you take out the trash on your way out please?

> (b) Take out the reference in your essay about Joey, he might not appreciate it.

Take After – To look or act like someone else

Wow, David really takes after his father. He looks and acts like him.

Take Over – To conquer or take control of something.

Do you want me to take over? You look tired.

Take Apart – To dismantle or reduce something or someone's action or statement

(a) Did you see the debate yesterday between the two candidates? The Senator took his opponent apart.

(b) I won't know what's wrong with your car until I take the motor apart.

Take In – To observe with detail and for enjoyment

We took in the view when we climbed the mountain

Take Up – To begin to do something or accept an offer

(a) Did you hear about Eric, I heard he took up scriptwriting and stopped writing novels.

(b) I think I'll take you up on that offer to go to Hawaii. I really need a break.

Take Back – To regret and apologize for something said or done

"Take it back! I never cheated in soccer. You were the one who always cries foul.

Make Out – To have intimate relationships with someone such as kissing.

I saw Jenny and Ted making out at the restaurant last night. I didn't know they were a couple.

Make of – To figure something out or to try and distinguish something.

What do you make of this painting? It's truly odd.

Make Over – To have a complete change in life or physical look

Laurie had a complete makeover while on vacation in the Bahamas

Make Through – To survive something or to complete something

Doctors said he's gonna make it through. He was shot in the chest, but it didn't hit any vital organs.

Chapter 2 - Going Beyond Hello

Learning Objectives

➡ Students will be able to describe themselves to others

➡ Students will be able to converse in short dialogues with others

➡ Students will be able to comprehend and discuss basic quotations and proverbs

➡ Students will be able to discuss and write about their experiences learning English

➡ Students will be able to use future tenses describing their goals and ambitions in life

➡ Students will be able to search and share stories relating to their backgrounds and experiences

➡ Students will be able to understand and use vocabulary regarding their backgrounds and experiences

Model the initial questions for the students by asking them to give you your own information and write on the board. Start with:

- "What's my name?

- How do you spell that?"

- What kind of music do you listen to?"

- "Where do you live?"

- "Where were you born?"

Once the students have responded, further model by having one student ask another the first three questions.

You can deploy this exercise in whatever way works best for your classroom at the moment: pairs, groups of three or four, a line-up, or whatever else works best for you. Be sure to have the students report back on their findings after the exercise.

This reporting reinforces a critical component of conversation, which is remembering what your partner or partners tell you and the ability to use the third person. For example:

- "She said that she likes traveling around the world"

- "He said that he was born in Sanaa, Yemen but raised in London."

- "She likes eating organic and locally grown food."

p. 12 Asking Questions

This activity gives your students an opportunity to reinforce their conversational skills by writing down questions. Remember that English skills are synergistic: the better your students are at reading and writing, the better conversationalists they will usually be.

p. 12 Paraphrasing Proverbs

Make sure your students know what the various attributed nationalities and ethnicities mean. Discuss how different cultures, nationalities and languages can produce different views and variations on the topics of the proverb. For example, Spanish uses the word "ganar," "to win," for earning money at a job. The English verb says that you "earn" money, the Spanish verb says that you "win" money. Why this difference, and what does this difference mean? See what your students have to say. See if you can find any similar comparisons in the other languages spoken by your students.

Sound Sense: Pronunciation Practice

When focusing on pronunciation practice, the final syllable is usually the least stressed in the English language (Unlike in Korea where it is emphasized). Nevertheless, the subtle differences between the sounds can produce different meanings altogether and therefore should be practices.

Minimal Pair for "Goal:" *Gall, gale, gull, pole, poll, hole, roll, role, toll, and mole.*

Pairing: *All and ail, small and snail, fall and fail, tall and tale.*

Ial/Ale	All/O	Ole/Oal
Gale	Gall	Goal
Jail	Jolly	Cajole
Pale	Paltry	Pole
Rail	Rob	Role
Snail	Snob	Sole
Stale	Stall	Stole

p. 15 Search and Share

A great way to introduce and model this activity is to perform it yourself, bringing in pictures of your own hometown, and answering all the questions about yourself for the students. This ice-breaker for the beginning of the school year is a good way to introduce yourself to your students as a prelude to their introducing themselves to each other.

p. 16 On your own

This activity is an opportunity for students to reflect and assess what they have learned by identifying areas that their own language differs from English. For example, Mandarin Chinese has no conjugations for past, present or future tense. The time of an action is determined from the context in a sentence. French does not use the present continuous tense. Spanish uses different tenses and conjugations for the subjunctive and the conditional. What other examples can you and your students come up with, and what do these differences mean to learning and expression in English? What advantages do more verb tenses and conjugations confer? Do they allow more possibility for expression in the language?

EXPANSION ACTIVITIES

Academic Vocabulary Expansion: Prefix/Suffix Study
Prefixes alluding to location: Inter/Intra

You can use a plethora of vocabulary using inter and intra. Show students how with the advent of new technology these two (and many other prefixes/suffixes) prefixes are used to create new words (Internet and Intranet). I personally like to combine English for Specific Purposes to students with topics such as technology. Many students already know what the internet is but few might know what intranet is. Refer them to companies such as Cisco Systems and how most major companies and institutions have a secure intranet system (such as the institute or college you work at) to ensure that only those specific people have access to the intranet system (username and password are the most common entry barriers). Another good example is the difference in the USA between interstate and intrastate (think highways, commerce, law, etc.). This would be a good government and English lesson when referring to the USA as a uniquely Federal system as opposed to most countries in the world.

> *Introvert, Intramural, intransitive, intrapersonal, intrastate.*
>
> *Intervene, interrupt, intercede, interlude, interoffice, intermission, intersection, interstate*

Phrasal Verbs

Come through, come up with, come again, come after, come for, come over, come off

The verb come is often used as a phrasal verb. Have students practice changing the prepositions to see how it impacts the meaning of the sentence. Use popular movies to show usage. For example: "I'm coming after you" used by Liam Neeson in the famous movie "Taken." Compare this to the simple form of come after such as dessert comes after the main course.

Come Through – To get something or a deal arranged or done

> We can finally buy that Saab car you always wanted. The loan came through.

Come Up With – An issue, situation, or problem that occurs or presents itself, especially unexpectedly

> Sorry, can't make it tonight (great phrasal verb as well), something came up at work.

Come Again – To repeat something that wasn't heard or understood

> Come again? I don't think I understood what your plan was.

Come After – To chase or try to get someone

> You better pay your student loans back, or they will come after you. They will even take or garnish your wages.

Come For – arrive to arrest or detain someone

> What happened to Joey? The cops came for him this morning. I guess he never paid back all those unpaid tickets.

Come Over – To change sides or views

> Looks like Mikey has finally came over to our side. He just quit his job and applied to our company.

Come Off – Used to express a statement or attitude that can seem insulting or controversial.

> Where do come off talking to me that way? You have some nerve! I never did any thing to you.

Come To – To wake up

> When he came to after the operation, he felt pain-free and happy.

Chapter 3 - Making and Breaking Habits

Learning Objectives

→ Students will be able to describe and discuss habits, schedules and routines

→ Students will be able to describe and write using "wh" questions

→ Students will be able to use adverbs of frequency to describe their routines and habits

→ Students will be able to search and share information pertaining to peoples' habits and routines

→ Students will be able to write basic paragraphs about their behaviors, lifestyles and practices

→ Students will be able to plan and discuss their schedules in English

Begin by introducing the topic. Define and discuss: What is a habit? What habits do you have? What are some good habits? What are some bad habits? Is practicing English a good habit or bad habit? How about smoking? How about brushing your teeth? Have your students explain why these habits are good or bad. Make sure you establish that a habit is a regular, routine activity that can be either good or bad.

You can carry this activity further by having students list their good and bad habits as a writing exercise, then pair them to exchange this information conversationally. Alternately, you can begin by pairing the students to interview each other about good and bad habits, with each student writing down the other's good and bad habits, then reporting these back to the class. This exchange is a good opportunity to introduce humor and fun into the English learning process. Maybe one student studies too much, another chews too much gum, another never speaks English outside of class...Make it fun!

Caution: Students who do not live in San Francisco or Santa Monica, California or similar cities may be confused by questions about paper, plastic and canvas bags. Explain the environmental concerns around these various products, and the utility of re-usable grocery bags. Define concepts such as "Farmer's Market" and "recycling center."

p. 17 Sharing Stories

Pair your students. Tell them to make sure to remember the answers of their partners, as each student will report back to the group about his partner's answers. You can further reinforce listening skills, memory and check comprehension by asking third person questions based on student answers. An example might be, "What did Maria eat for breakfast today?" You may do this either immediately after the exercise or later in the session.

Minimal pairs for "die:" *day, due, tie, lie, buy, guy, eye, my, pie.*

p. 19 Asking Questions

Review the listed question words with the students and make sure all of your students understand the meaning and use of such question words as who, what, when, why, where and how.

p. 20 The Conversation Continues

Caution: This section has some questions that can be perceived and received by some as negative or critical. For example, your students may have different views on smoking. Such instances are best taken as opportunities for the teacher to delineate conversation norms in the United States and how to express differing opinions in a respectful, considerate way. If a disagreement arises on a topic, guide your students away from an argument and to a respectful difference of opinion, emphasizing an open-minded spirit of inquiry.

For example, ask the students why the United States now has so many restrictions on smoking, from restaurants and public places even to a ban on television advertising of tobacco products. Why are countries like France, China and Vietnam so much less concerned with the health issues of smoking than people in the United States? These techniques can turn a potential problem or uncomfortable situation into a great opportunity for intercultural exchange. It can also enhance the learning experience if you make it clear that the teacher is also learning.

p. 22-23 Search and Share

You can begin this section as a writing exercise, and then pair or group the students to exchange their information. You can also begin by pairing or grouping the students and having them interview each other for the information and write it down. In either instance, you can have partners report their findings back to the whole group.

Sound Sense: Pronunciation Practice

Many English language learners have difficulty in pronouncing the final s sounds. Have students practice the final s sounds with those that do not. Extend the exercise by having students practice the difference between the final s sound as a Z or S ending depending on the final consonant or vowel. This is a good chapter to teach the voice and voiceless consonants and how they determine the s sound endings.

This is a good opportunity to assess students' own languages. For example, Koreans seem to overstress the last letter while Italians do not have a final consonant on their words.

Long A Sound	Long A with Z sound at the end
Day	Days
Delay	Delays
Pay	Pays
Tray	Trays
Way	Ways

EXPANSION ACTIVITIES

Academic Vocabulary Expansion: Prefix/Suffix Study
Prefixes Super and Over/Under

> *Superstitious, superintendent, superiority, supervise*

Great discussion starter would be to ask if students are superstitious or what superstitions come from their cultures.

For the more advanced students:

> *Superfluous, supersede, superimpose, superlative*

This exercise could be a great segment to delve into adjectives of comparison using comparative and superlative more/less/most/least and er/est. One great hint is using the number six for students when they try to figure out whether or not to use er/est or more/less/most/least.

Example: Happy has five letters, therefore happier and happiest. Handsome has eight letters therefore more/less and most least handsome.

The prefix "over" is used quite commonly and therefore is a great way to teach students not to be afraid of words that have many letters. Instead, have students break down words according to prefixes and suffixes and for the more advanced students include roots and stems.

Examples:

Overthink, overestimate vs. underestimate, overdue, overdrawn, over

The following can be used for both "over" and "under":

> *pay*
> *done*
> *dose*
> *eat*
> *drawn*
> *estimate*
> *achiever*
> *populated*
> *rate*
> *worked*

Phrasal Verbs
Make/do

One of the most useful (and most confusing) of the phrasal verbs are those using make and do. I have often used an entire class hour just going over these two. One of my favorite examples is make up. This phrasal verb has several meanings and it drives students crazy.

[Make Up has several meanings from make up a test or make up an appointment to make up a story. It's extremely confusing for students and therefore very useful to teach.]

Make Up – To reschedule or do something again

Mark, you need to make up the test you missed if you want to pass my class.

Make Up – Direct phrase meaning to decide

Can you make up your mind already, I'm starving! Just choose something already.

Do (something) over– do again.

You didn't get a good grade on the homework assignment. You need to do it over.

Do (someone) in– kill someone (real or imaginary).

The robbers tried to steal my money and then do me in.

Do (someone) good– be good for someone.

I know you don't want to learn Latin, but it will do you good in the future.

Do without (something)– live without something.

We didn't bring enough money to the store so we are going to have to do without the snacks.

Do away with– stop having something.

The school is going to do away with uniforms. Nobody likes them.

Do well for (oneself)– become successful.

Danny has really done well for himself. He owns 5 restaurants.

SIDEBAR: Make vs. Do

What do you do? What do you make?

These simple words cause lots of confusion for English language learners. Both intermediate and advanced English language learners struggle with the difference between "make" and "do". We have so many different idioms and expressions that use these two hard-working, common verbs.

Here is a quick, imprecise guide that helps clarify the issue.

Look at some common expressions with "do".

> Do the dishes.
> Do some chores.
> Do your work.
> Do exercises.
> Do your best.
> Do it over.
> Do the report.

Do is used to describe an activity that you have to do, often over and over again. For instance, we "do the dishes" and "do the laundry" many times. Do also contains an element of duty and responsibility.

Now, take a look at some expressions with "make".

> Please make time.
> You make dinner.
> You make drawings.
> You make decisions.
> You make plans.
> Your make reservations.
> You make money.
> You make friends.

Make is used to describe a creative activity or something you choose to do. You choose, for instance, to make plans, make friends, and make decisions. You have choices.

Why do we say "make dinner" if we have to do it over and over? Perhaps because cooking is seen more as a creative activity than a chore. But cleaning the table, and cleaning the dishes are just chores so we say "do the table" and "do the dishes." That's also why Americans say "make money" instead of "do money." Making money is seen as both creative and a choice. Learning this expression illuminates how the United States remains a strong consumer culture – even in the most common expressions.

Sometimes we forget how much cultural information can be contained in short sayings and everyday idioms. Sometimes Americans will use the verb "make" in a way that might seem strange to English students. Many students have noted that they don't choose to "make mistakes" on their exams! Still, English students usually "make a decision" to "do their best" and "make progress" in learning our confusing language.

Finally, encourage students to work together in small groups and create their own list of idioms and phrases with make and do. If you have time, ask students to come to the white board and write their collection of idioms on the board. This communicative activity remains surprisingly popular semester after semester. Homework, of course, is asking them to choose 5-10 idioms and write complete sentences.

So how do you teach the difference between do and make to your English students?

Chapter 4 - Studying English

Learning Objectives

→ Students will be able to interview and respond to questions concerning second language acquisition

→ Students will be able to understand basic vocabulary used to describe second language acquisition

→ Students will be able to recognize common idioms and expressions

→ Students will be able to use do/does/did questions and respond appropriately both in conversation and writing

→ Students will be able to comprehend present perfect questions and respond appropriately both in conversation and writing

→ Students will be able to understand how and which questions and respond appropriately both in conversation and writing

→ Students will be able to discuss topics relating to driving in the United States

→ Students will be able to converse about different social media outlets in their home country and in the United States

→ Students will be able to search and share pronunciation tips in English such as common word stress patterns and certain sounds

When raising and exploring the confusing aspects of learning English as a second language, you can begin by asking the students what is most confusing about learning the language for them. What about English is most different from their native language? Your understanding of your individual students' experience with their native languages will enhance your understanding of them and their needs in learning English.

Explain and explore the meaning of "bilingual." Explain that all of your students are now by definition bilingual, as they speak English in addition to their native language. Depending on your student population, you might also want to explain that some of your students might now be multi-lingual and/or poly-lingual. Even if you are teaching "ESL," English may actually be their third, fourth or fifth language. For example, common combinations are Russian, Ukrainian and English or Spanish, English, and a pre-Columbian tribal language such as Zapotec, Chinanteco, Meji, Quiche, etc. You can also explore how students coming into your class as native (or more recent) bilinguals can use this experience to help them learn English. We prefer the relatively rare term "English as an Additional Language" for its accuracy.

Idioms - p. 26

Explain to your students the concept and uses of idioms, as slang, street talk, casual speech, etc. Ask your students to name places where they are likely to encounter idioms. Explain where idioms are not used, such as in formal writing. Explain the difference between a literal expression and a metaphoric or figurative expression. If you have willing students, you can even act these expressions out. For example, you can ask, if I say I'm pulling your leg, am I actually pulling on your leg? Is this expression literal or figurative?

Go through all of the idioms with similar questions: If your boss was angry and yelled at you, did she literally jump down your throat? While snakes can swallow whole animals, human beings cannot. These examples should illustrate for your students the crucial skills for defining and understanding idioms.

The Conversation Continues - p. 26

Make sure to use follow-up questions here, either by asking them yourself, or encouraging your students to ask their partners. If they eavesdropped on a conversation, what did they hear? What did they wish they had not heard?

Discussing Quotations - p. 26-27

Culture Connection: You can tie in this section with lessons on some of the historical figures quoted, such as Martin Luther King, John F. Kennedy or Ronald Reagan. In the case of Martin Luther King, Jr., the lesson can also be coordinated with the holiday celebrating King's birthday.

Search and Share - P. 29

This activity can be performed in a computer lab if you and your class have access to one. If you do not have access to such a facility, you can have students use their smartphones, tablets and other devices to find these videos on the internet. Monitor practice closely or you may find that your students are watching cartoons or dogs on bicycles rather than following the lesson guidelines.

Sound Sense: Pronunciation Practice

Minimal pairs for "eat:" *beat, seat, treat, feet, feat, neat, heat, meet, meat, wheat, greet, feet, feat, cheat, back seat, brow beat, delete, upbeat.*

This is a great pronunciation practice for the short and long vowels. Many languages already have short vowels that do not require much facial movement. We like to actually demonstrate this to students by noting that the human face has 46 muscles. This allows for flexibility of sounds, specifically when it comes to American English.

The long vowel sounds are the issue for many students and do result in miscommunication for students.

Have students practice the longer vowel sounds using the words above as opposed to shorter sounds such as sit, it, bit, hit, grit, etc.

Here is a practice set. Have students create some in class or on the board:

Short i sound	Long e sound
It	Eat
Bit	Beat
Hit	Heat
Grit	Greet
Sit	Seat
Fit	Feat/Feet
Lit	Delete

Expansion Activities

Academic Vocabulary Expansion: Prefix/Suffix Study
Prefixes for numbers

> **1 = Mono/uni**
>> *Monologue, monotone, monogamy, monopoly*
>
> **2 = Dia/Bi**
>> *Dialogue, diameter, diagonal, diatribe, bicycle, bipolar, bilateral.*
>
> **3 = Tri**
>> *Tristate, triple, trilingual, trilateral, tricycle, triceps.*
>
> **4 = Quad**
>> *Quadruped, quadrupled, quad (as in an open space between four buildings).*
>
> **5 = Pent/quint**
>> *Pentagon, pentacle, pentagram, pentangle*
>
> **6 = Hex**
>> *Hexagon, hexachord*
>
> **7 = Sept/hept**
>> *Heptagon*
>
> **8 = Oct**
>> *Octopus, octagon, octuplets*
>
> **9 = Nov**
>
> **10 = Dec**
>> *Decade, decathlon*

The list above can be a great exercise to show students how the numerical prefixes can be added to a list of words they already know.

Some easy words to practice with: Unicycle, bicycle, tricycle; unilingual, bilingual, trilingual; quad lingual.

Phrasal Verbs

There are many phrasal verbs with the verb "to bring." Therefore, it is worth mentioning to your students about this verb. Here are some examples:

Bring about — To cause something to happen:

> 'The 1960s youth movement brought about a change in American culture and politics.'

Bring around — To change someone's view or opinion

> 'I used to eat meat until I saw a TV show on vegetarianism which really brought me around.'

Bring back — To take back or return something

> 'Can you bring back the book I lent you?'
> 'They should bring back smoking in bars. I hate going outside to smoke.'

Bring down — To fall or collapse

> 'The Berlin Wall was brought down in 1989.'

Bring off — To succeed at something difficult/ to accomplish something that seemed impossible

> 'I can't believe your wife let you come with us. How did you bring that off?'

Bring on — Very similar to bring about mentioned above. To cause something to appear

> 'The strong smell of flowers brought on sneezing from her. She's allergic to them.'

Bring out — To come out / release:

> 'My favorite author is bringing out a new book next month.'

Bring out (2) — To stress or to highlight something

> 'That make-up really brings out your eyes.'

Bring to — To revive consciousness

> 'The doctor used a strong smelling salts to bring to the boxer after he had been knocked out.'

Bring up — To mention

> 'I'd like to bring up an important point about this issue.'

Chapter 5 - Being Yourself
....

Learning Objectives

→ Students will be able to share points of view with their classmates

→ Students will be able to delve deeper into their characteristics such as personality traits and cultural differences

→ Students will be able to use vocabulary relating to personality traits and characteristics describing people

→ Students will be able to talk about adjectives describing people characters and behaviors

→ Students will be able to paraphrase (both writing and speaking) proverbs and quotations and discuss them with others

→ Students will be able to ask and answer questions about proverbs and quotations

→ Students will be able to search and share videos relating to individual characteristics and behaviors

Define and clarify the meaning and uses of the words in the questions on page 31. Make sure the students understand what they mean and how they are used. Explore the derivation of these words as terms for personal characteristics. For example, you can bring in materials such as wood, rubber, metal, etc. to demonstrate the physical meaning of words such as "rigid" versus "flexible," and how these words transfer metaphorically to describe human characteristics.

p. 33 Paraphrasing Proverbs

In exploring these proverbs with your students, tie them in with where you live and the daily life of you and your students. For example, if you live and work in a city like Los Angeles, California, explore how the cars people own and drive can define their identities, social status, and the impressions they make on other people. Conversely, if you live and work in a city like Hong Kong, London or New York, you can inquire into how an absence of cars in commuting and daily use affects relations between people. How does everyday interaction change when people commute inside their cars versus when they rub shoulders (explain idiom) on trains and buses?

p. 34 The Conversation Continues

A great way to expand and reinforce the exercise in this section is to have the students list the characteristics they identify and then write them on the board. This expansion activity is a good opportunity for a seamless integration between conversation, reading and writing. Once the lists of characteristics are on the board, you can further the conversation by asking the students more questions. Are any that they disagree with? Are there any they would add? Why? Are there any that they personally wish they had more or less of? Use your own imagination and experience to further the conversation.

p. 36 Search and Share

Feel free to narrow the focus of this exercise if you want your students to find a video on a specific topic related to other aspects of your lessons and class.

Caution: Emphasize to your students that the videos they find and use must be in English. This may seem obvious, and doubtlessly will be to many of your students. However, if you do not state this guideline pre-emptively, you may find yourself being talked through Spanish-language soap operas by students who didn't quite understand the purpose of the assignment.

Caution: p. 37 - While the question asked of the students is phrased in a very positive manner, don't be surprised if from time to time you might get very negative answers. Students can occasionally reveal emotional problems and other personal issues in their written and even conversational responses to such exercises. It is best to follow the guidelines of your school in referring students for further help that they may need. Keep in mind that teaching and counseling are two very separate skills and professions. Don't hesitate to refer students to the help and resources available in your school and community.

Sound Sense: Pronunciation Practice

Short a sound	Longer a sound	Longest a sound
All	An	Lane
Ball	Ban	Bane
Call	Can	Cane
Fall	Fan	Faint
Hall	Hand	Hail
Mall	Man	Main

Expansion Activities

Academic Vocabulary Expansion: Prefix/Suffix Study
Suffix: less/full, ive, y, ly

The y and ly ending usually indicate either adjective or adverb. This is a way to teach grammatical information that gives students a better way to determine the structure of the word. When a word ends in a consonant plus "Y" then the "Y" is changed to "I" when you add the suffix. When adding the suffix 'ing' to a word ending in "Y" -- you keep the "Y."

> lonely + ness = *loneliness*
> happy + ness = *happiness*
> copy + ing   = *copying*

Silent "E" words end with a consonant and an "E." Words like love, like, and hope... you drop the "E" when you add the suffix.

$$noise + y = \textit{noisy}$$
$$simple + y = \textit{simply}$$

Phrasal Verbs

Call is also widely used with prepositions to create phrasal verbs. Play close attention to those with multiple meanings.

Call up/off/from

Call after - be named after someone

> He was called Joe after his uncle who had died in the war.

Call around – Visit

> I'll call you around 1 o'clock in the afternoon.

Call back – Return a phone call

> You better call John back. He's called twice already.

Call for – A) demand; B) phone call; C) require; D) pick me up from a certain place

> A) There's not much call for refrigerators in the Arctic Circle.
> B) Did you call for an appointment?
> C) This good news calls for a celebration!
> D) He called for her at home but she wasn't there last night.

Call In – get someone to come and do something.

> We had to call in a plumber because our drain was clogged.

Call off – To cancel

> The reunion was called off because not enough people could attend.

Chapter 6 - Choosing and Keeping Friends

Learning Objectives

➡ Students will be able to discuss and share memories using past tense and conditionals

➡ Students will be able to research, read, review and cite sources from articles online

➡ Students will be able to draw vocabulary from articles and use them in their writing and speaking

➡ Students will be able to write and talk about an article they have read online

➡ Students will be able to write a letter or email to a friend describing their experiences

➡ Converse with general clarity using pronunciation/stress/ intonation patterns

Introduce and/or review the concept of "friends." Describe and delineate the difference between acquaintances, family and friends. You can do an exercise in writing, conversation or both to have students list the people in their lives and how they fit in these three categories. You can model this by doing your own list on the board, in a handout, on the projector or using any medium you think best fits your current lesson. You can also list people twice, or draw lines to illustrate how people can fit into more than one category. For example, your sister might also be one of your best friends.

Minimal pair for "Friend:" *Trend, bend, mend, fend, lend, send, end, tend, vend.*

p. 40 Asking Questions

Define and explore the differences between friends and family. How are these two groups the same? How can they can be different? What is meant by the American saying, "You can choose your friends, but you can't choose your family." Why do some people look forward to spending time with their families during holidays and other occasions, while others feel nothing but dread at the approach of these same events? You can expand the conversation by exploring the topic of when and how friendships begin, continue, and sometimes end. This aspect can also be used to introduce or expand the "Paraphrasing Proverbs" exercise on p. 40.

p. 41 The Conversation Continues

Introduction and modeling will help students with some concepts in this section that might be unfamiliar. Explain what it means to "betray" a friend. You can use examples from real life, news events, movies, television…even Shakespeare, depending on the level and background of your class. You can also explain and model by using examples from your own life. Have you, the teacher, ever been betrayed by someone? What do you, the teacher, do to keep your friendships strong?

p. 43 - Search and Share

Caution: Take into account the relative ages of your students in order to assess their relationship to the internet and social media. Older students might never have used these technologies; younger students might never have known life without them. You can vary this assignment according to the backgrounds and needs of your students. Perhaps a student completely unfamiliar with social media could be assigned to create an account with you or another student in the class. Much as you pair students by skill level and language background, you can also pair internet newcomers with students already comfortable with social media.

Caution: Younger students accustomed to social media may not know what a postcard is. Explain the differences between letters, postcards and emails. You can show examples of each to the class to illustrate your explanation.

Sound Sense: Pronunciation Practice

Short e sound	Short a sound	More advanced words
Bend	Band	Benevolent
Blend	Bland	Expand
End	And	Depend
Lend	Land	Splendid
Send	Sand	Transcend
Spend	Span	Overspend

Show how adding the ending "er" can often describe one who does this activity or job. However, this rule does not always work for every words.

Expansion Activities

Academic Vocabulary Expansion Prefix/Suffix Study:
Word Form: Suffix
Able/ible, describe, script, er/ar/ist/eer/or/cian

Teach the suffixes using the words from the pronunciation pair to demonstrate "one who"

Have the students practice by looking for ending of words that and adding these suffixes. Here is a possible exercise for these:

sail_____	invent _____
direct_____	magic _____
audit_____	electric _____
edit _____	music_____
tail _____	mathematic_____(doctor of mathematics)

Phrasal Verbs

Instead of teaching individual phrasal verbs, choose a theme and teach all the possible phrasal verbs that relate to it. The example below relates to relationships between people.

Depend on, count on, rely on, and latch onto. Opposite ones would be put up with, drift apart, split up.

Chapter 7 - Playing and Watching Sports

Learning Objectives

→ Students will be able to have a conversation about sports and leisure in the United States

→ Students will be able to compare and contrast sports in the United States with their countries

→ Students will learn vocabulary related to sports and be able to use them in conversations

→ Students will review and discuss expressions relating to sports and leisure

→ Students will be able to construct and answer questions relating to sports and leisure

→ Students will be able to search and share information regarding sports using popular American sports websites

→ Students will be able to research, write and describe professional athletes to their classmates

You can introduce this topic by bringing in various sports implements and gear, either full-scale or children's toys. You can also use a picture dictionary.

A good way to explore and define these sports is to explore why some sports like soccer, basketball and martial arts are popular on a global level, while others like (American) football remain stubbornly local. You can also introduce the subject by asking your students why people play sports. What makes a great athlete? How do people, particularly children, benefit from playing sports? Can people become too preoccupied with sports? How preoccupied with sports are Americans versus people in other countries? Why do athletes, and sometimes countries, cheat at sports?

Caution: The terminology and nomenclature of sports can get confusing at times, both for teachers and students. The sport known in the United States as soccer is known everywhere else in the world (including the English-speaking world of Britain, Australia and elsewhere) as "football." The sport known in the United States as football is known elsewhere in the world as "American football." Some students further this confusion by referring to "football soccer" when they are talking about soccer. It is best to clarify these terms and definitions at the outset, or you can end up spending a lot of time in conversation disentangling what sports you and your students are actually talking about. Hint: pictures can be very helpful, and they are very easily obtained. Simply take the sports page of your local newspaper and show the students pictures of athletes playing football and soccer. You can also use pictures from the internet for this purpose.

Caution: It is also good to go over and review sports events like the Olympics and in particular the Super Bowl, as the Super Bowl is a uniquely American event for this uniquely American sport. You may be surprised to find that many students have little awareness of the Olympics and the Super Bowl.

Minimal pair for "fan:" *fun, pan, man, ban, tan, can, ran, van.*

p. 47 Grammar Connection

Review question words. This can tie in with grammar lessons involving questions in simple present and past tense.

p. 47 Vocabulary Connection

The sports chapter is a great place to include action verbs such as throw, hit, jump, kick, etc.

p. 47 - The Conversation Continues

Discuss the relationship between physical and mental effort and activity in a sport. How do mental strength and concentration bring victory through physical achievement? How does this connection contribute to other areas of life? Why do some superstar (explain idiom) athletes become very accomplished in other fields as well? Examples include Arnold Schwarzenegger (world champion bodybuilder to #1 movie star to businessman to politician as twice-elected governor of California), Magic Johnson (Los Angeles Lakers basketball star to businessman, entrepreneur and team owner of the Los Angeles Dodgers baseball team), Oscar de la Hoya (Olympic and professional champion boxer to entrepreneur and professional) Tony Hawk (champion skateboarder to entrepreneur, businessman, promoter and philanthropist) and Mike "Mouse" McCoy (Champion motorcycle racer to film producer and director, entrepreneur and businessman).

p. 48 - Idioms and Paraphrasing Sayings

You can expand this exercise by adding additional idioms. Feel free to include these or any other examples you can think of:

"fumble a pass,"
"out of bounds,"
"off the wall,"
"keep your eye on the ball,"/"keep your eyes on the prize,"
"take the ball and run with it,"
"hog the ball,"
"fast break,"
"lay down,"
"throw the game,"
"hit a home run,"
"hit it out of the park,"
"Three strikes you're out"
"off-base,"/"get past first base"
  *(not in an amorous sense)
"Out in left field,"
"Touch 'em all,"
"hit below the belt,"
"knockout,"
"slap shot,"
"throw elbows,"
"rally"
"fix a game,"
"spike the football,"
"victory dance,"

"sack dance,"
"no pain, no gain,"
"work through the pain,"
"shrug off the pain,
"pump it up,/"sweat it out,"/"jump through hoops,"
"bad call,"/"good call"
"teamwork,"/"not on the same team,"/"playing for the other team,"
"(not) play ball with someone,"
"raise/lower the bar,"
"down to the wire,"
"cross the finish line,"
"bet on the wrong horse,"
"rough seas/waters"
"smooth sailing,"
"adrift"
"capsize,"
"odd man out"
"pick a winner,"
"off to the races,"
"jump the gun,"
"time out,"
"in the arena,"
"the nosebleed section,"/"the cheap seats,"

"soccer hooligan,"   "big boy's rules"
"benchwarmer,"/"second/third string,"   "major league,"
"little league"   "bush league"
"catch the wave,"   "play with the pros,"
"surf the wave"   "bulls eye,"
"wipeout,"   "hit/miss the target"
"strike out,"   "on target"
"batting a thousand,"   "belly flop"
"choke,"   "off the deep end"
"balk,"
"on steroids,"
"contact sport" (e.g. "politics is a
contact sport)

It is also productive to explain how many of these expressions can be both affirmative and negative. For example, you can say, "He wasn't exactly batting a thousand at work today" or "He didn't play ball with me on that contract."

It's also fun and productive to explore the different meanings and ramifications that many of these idioms can have (within the bounds of classroom propriety, of course). For example, a literal "knockout" refers to a blow in boxing or other contact sports that causes unconsciousness. However, a "knockout" can refer to a complete triumph with a presentation, business or other activity. (The salesman's pitch to his customers was a knockout). It can also refer to an exceptionally attractive person. (The new secretary at our office is a real knockout.) Explain to your students the derivation of these various uses: a knockout in boxing is a complete, absolute, instant victory, an unqualified triumph. Conversely, the sight of an exceptionally handsome or beautiful person can make you feel like you've taken leave of your senses, like you've been knocked out.

Similarly, "work through the pain" has a literal meaning in weightlifting or bodybuilding of going through the stress and effort of lifting heavy weights in order to achieve gains in size and strength. This expression also refers to going through the work of less enjoyable tasks to achieve the rewards of starting a business, learning a new language, and other rewarding pursuits.

p. 48-49 Discussing Quotations

"Winning isn't everything. It's the only thing." - Vince Lombardi, football coach. What does he mean by this? Why would winning be the only thing? How does this philosophy play out in other areas of life besides sports?

> "A man may make mistakes, but he is not a failure until he starts blaming some one else."
>
> — John Wooden

You can have the students guess the meanings, and then group them to compose and write sentences using the idioms. Students love English idioms, and you will find that students often pick them up (explain idiom) and use them right away in class.

p. 48 Vocabulary Connection

These idioms are also a great opportunity to explore and review action verbs. Many picture dictionaries have good sections illustrating the various actions in sports: Throw, catch, hit, run, fall, slide, serve, spike, etc.

p. 48 Search and Share

Caution: Make sure your students understand that this activity is to find an article in English. Your students may protest that the team or athlete they are searching for is Italian, Spanish, Brazilian, etc., so be prepared to respond that regardless of the nationality or native language of the athletes in question, the article(s) about them must be in English.

Explain and illustrate the concept of rivalry. This activity is a good opportunity to construct your own lesson and bring in your own real-world experiences of famous rivalries from sports and other arenas. Some examples from recent decades that can be fascinating to revisit are Muhammad Ali and "Gentleman" Joe Frazier, Billie Jean King and Chris Everett, and Larry Bird and Michael Jordan. Some of these famous rivalries also bring opportunities to explore the cultural, ethnic and racial issues that sometimes emerge around the sports rivalries. Feel free to make use of the abundance of books, newspaper and magazine articles, and video around these famous sports rivalries. Make sure to practice vocabulary and check comprehension, using student vocabulary to describe what they see in pictures and videos.

An opponent is anyone against whom one is competing. A rivalry, though, is an especially intense competition against an opponent one has met many times. You can expand the concept of rivalry to other areas such as politics. In American history, Alexander Hamilton and Aaron Burr were famous rivals. Abe Lincoln and Stephen Douglas were famous rivals. Can your students provide other examples of political rivals? Other types of rivalry involve competing for the same job, the same boyfriend or the same girlfriend, or for coveted rewards such as best insurance salesman.

Sound Sense: Pronunciation Practice

An Ending	And Ending	Ang Ending
An	And	Bang
Ban	Band	Boomerang
Han	Hand	Hang/Overhang
Man	Demand	Mango
Ran	Rand	Rang

This is a good opportunity to discuss with students the importance of listening for meaning. The most important thing is to focus on meaning rather than having to know each word that was spoken.

Academic Vocabulary Expansion: Prefix/Suffix Study

Suffix Endings for Nouns (from verbs)

A great and quick way to increase students' vocabulary is to teach the suffix ending for nouns. Students can practice with verbs they know and try to form nouns with them. For example, have them match the following suffixes with the following verbs:

tion, cion, sion, ment

Establish _____

Notate _____

Locate _____

Dictate _____

Immerse _____

Dedicate _____

Coerce _____

Cohabitate _____

Develop _____

Embellish _____

Phrasal Verb

Go for/after/in, on

Go off− to make a loud noise or to explode.

> My alarm clock went off at 7:00 a.m.

Go over− to review.

> You should go over your homework before you give it to the teacher. Make sure there are no mistakes.

Go on– to happen.

> What is going on in Brazil right now?

Go with– to match, to be similar to.

> I like your scarf. It goes with your dress.

Go out– (1) to stop working (machines or electrical things).

> The power went out last night just as we were watching the horror movie.

Go out– (2) to be a part of a social activity.

> I'm going out tonight, don't wait up.

Go out– (3) to date someone.

> Did you hear? Ashton is going out with Mila.

Go along with– to agree with or follow.

> Joey usually goes along with what the boss says. He's old-school (Great idiom to teach).

Go by– to pass.

> Three hours went by. Or I will go by that old house.

Chapter 8 - Talking about American Television

Learning Objectives

→ Students will be able to describe American television shows and practice conversations using vocabulary relating to American television.

→ Students will be able to describe their television viewing habits using the adverbs of frequency

→ Students will be able to write a short essay using the "wh" questions and the vocabulary from the chapter

→ Students will be able to demonstrate effective word usage when discussing preferences such as television genres

→ Students will be able to read and discuss quotations concerning entertainment

→ Students will be able to preview and recap what they saw regarding videos online relating to popular American television shows and movies

→ Students will be able to rate and review videos relating to American television shows

Caution: Depending on your student population, some may have studied English in countries where they learned British spellings, such as programme for the American program. Be aware of these possible differences and use them as opportunities to highlight the differences in written and spoken English among different countries and continents. You can point out that every widely-spoken language has these variations: Spanish used in Spain differs from Spanish used in Mexico; French in Paris differs from French in Montreal; English in London differs from English in New York City.

Minimal pair for "Fame:" *Shame, tame, lame, dame, came, game, maim, name.*

Caution: Introduce and explain vocabulary for American television such as drama, sitcom (situation comedy), and soap opera. Be aware that the Spanish-language term for soap opera is novela, so Spanish-speaking students will inevitably think the term in English is novel. You can explain that the word "novel" in English is actually a word for a book-length work of fiction, a long story as opposed to a short story. Depending on the level of your students, you can risk additional complication by explaining that in English a "novella" is a short novel. Similarly, French and Italian refer to a novel as roman and romanza, respectively. Depending on your student population, you can highlight the difference that a "romance" is actually a word for a particular genre of story, a love story.

Explain the derivation of the term soap opera, from the soap companies that originally sponsored the radio and television broadcasts of soap operas.

It will be helpful to explore the differences in formats between the television of the United States and other countries. Don't assume your students are necessarily familiar with terms like series, mini-series, reality show, and rerun. Explain that American television is usually formatted in terms of weekly series that continue stories until they are cancelled or "go off the air" (explain idiom). A series presents a certain number of new "episodes" for each "television season." A mini-series is a longer story with a definite ending that is presented in several "parts" or segments.

"Television serials" are much more common in Britain and other countries. For example, the Latin American "telenovelas" are long serials that end at a defined point that resolves the conflict and the fate of the characters. In contrast, American soap operas continue for many years and often decades through different communication mediums until the "show" is finally "cancelled." Many American soap operas began as radio programs, transferred to television shows and are now migrating to the internet when they have been cancelled from broadcast television. You can explain that "cancelled" in American television means that the broadcast network has decided that not enough people are watching the show to justify continuing the expense of producing it and broadcasting it.

There is a further opportunity here to present and discuss the differences between broadcast and cable television and the growing medium of internet TV. You can ask students what the big networks and television companies are in their own countries. For example, in

Mexico television is dominated by TV Azteca and Televisa. Interestingly, Univision, the largest Spanish-language network on American television, is an American company based in Miami, Florida.

The Brave and the Bold: An interesting topic to explore, while maintaining appropriate boundaries and classroom propriety, is what exactly is allowed in different mediums of television. For example, American broadcast television has evolved to the point of permitting the portrayal of tremendous amounts of often very gruesome violence, while still prohibiting profanity and nudity. In contrast, British television has a more relaxed attitude towards profanity and nudity, while prohibiting explicit violence.

You can also ask the students to explore such topics as why extended shootouts, horribly mutilated bodies and other manifestations of extreme violence are now regular staples of American broadcast television.The broadcast series "CSI" routinely shows horribly burned, mutilated and/or dismembered bodies in a way that was unknown in broadcast television even ten years ago. Is this increase in violence and mayhem because of an attempt to compete with non-broadcast television? What levels of violence, profanity and/or nudity do your students think is acceptable on TV? Why are many Americans so fascinated with this relatively gruesome and extreme material? Does violence seen on television cause some people to act out violence in real life?

This discussion is a great opportunity for students to express opinions in a classroom context that is open to and respectful of the views and experiences of students from many different countries and backgrounds. If you are brave enough to open a discussion with your students on these topics, you may be fascinated by what you find. For example, while many countries exercise more restraint in their popular culture than Americans do, countries like Japan, China and Italy actually have traditionally had more violence in their popular entertainment than Americans do. Some countries such as China and Saudi Arabia even televise public executions!

This lesson can also be an opportunity to explain and explore the role of paid advertising in American commercial television and compare it to the "telly license" subscriber system of public sponsorship in countries like Britain. What are the commercial and legal pressures on American broadcast television? How do these differ from the use of advertising sponsorship and federally-regulated public airwaves in some other countries? How do the pressures on regular broadcasting differ from those which are experienced by cable and satellite television, which are funded by subscriber payments? How has the fact that cable and satellite have an almost unlimited number of channels changed regular American TV? How has the fact that cable and satellite TV have vast freedom for the material they present changed regular TV programming?

The Conversation Continues p. 55: You can expand the conversation with the following questions: How realistic is television? How do stories and shows on television differ from how people behave and events unfold in real life? How real is "reality television?" Has playing video games made violence seem like entertainment?

Conversation Expansion Activity

Ask students about the nature of fame in modern America.

- Why do people want to be famous?

- Which is better, being famous or being rich?

- What's the difference between famous and infamous? Examples?

- Would you like to be famous? What are the advantages of being famous?

- What are the disadvantages?

- How many of each can you list?

- What is "reality television?"

- How real is it, in reality?

- Is "reality television" popular in the students' countries of origin?

- Why do people want to be on reality television?

- Would you want to be on reality TV?

- Would you want someone in your family to be on reality TV?

Students can be partnered for these questions, or you can ask them of the whole class. You can also use these extra questions as a continuation activity for more advanced students who finish the other questions first.

p. 55 Discussing Quotations

Quotes - "Television is chewing gum for the eyes." - Frank Lloyd Wright, Architect. Do you agree? Disagree? Why?

Depending on the backgrounds of your students, you may want to explore these quotations with a couple of preparatory exercises. Have students look through the quotations as a pre-reading exercise to search for new vocabulary words, if any. You might also want to go through the quotations to make sure the students understand what exactly is being expressed.

Do not assume that students will have any familiarity with some of the references made. For example, in the Bill Gates quotation, make sure your students understand that what Gates is referring to is the discrepancy between how characters behave in television shows and how real people behave in real life. In this case, Gates is talking about how characters on some television shows who are supposed to be adults living independently somehow never have to go to work or do anything to support themselves. The most likely example of this (and possibly the inspiration for Gates's comment) is the popular American television show "Friends," which shows the characters spending enormous amounts of time in a coffee shop socializing.

Other quotations from (Groucho) Marx, Welles and Hayakawa reflect an American cultural bias, or perhaps resistance, against television that existed through the second half of the 20th century as television embedded itself in the American culture. You can write the quotation from Frank Lloyd Wright on the board to introduce this idea. You can also use it to warm up and introduce your conversation exercises.

- What does Wright mean by this?

- Is chewing gum a productive, constructive activity?

- How about watching TV?

- Was this bias against television simply because it was new, or because it was supplanting older and perhaps more substantive mediums of communication such as books, theater and film?

- Does this bias still exist?

- Why has no similar bias about the internet emerged?

- How do the students feel about watching TV?

- Is it a waste of time, or does it offer opportunities for learning?

This might be a good place to suggest to your students that, if nothing else, watching TV in English has tremendous value for improving vocabulary and listening skills.

As a breakout sub-topic, you can explore the difference between "films," "movies" and TV. Why "films" would be considered an "art form" while television is often considered "trash?" What are the similarities and differences between films and television, e.g. physical size of presentation ("up on the big screen"), financing, paying for the experience (i.e. buying a ticket vs. watching commercials), subject matter, quality, etc. Are these differences growing or shrinking? How relevant are these differences?

You can also explore Oprah Winfrey as a cultural figure. Why is someone viewed as important and influential in people's lives simply because she is a successful television host? An example might be to play for your students Oprah's endorsement of Barack Obama as a presidential candidate in 2008.

- Is what she is saying rational or emotional?

- Why would people think a television celebrity's political endorsement was important in a democracy?

- Why are professional basketball players used in car ads?

- Can you think of other examples of celebrities in ads?

- Do you think such ads have impact?

Citizenship Connection: If you want, you can introduce that the United States Constitution specifically prohibits conferring any title of royalty or nobility onto any American citizen. Despite this, there is a lingering and well-noted tendency in American culture for books, newspapers and other media to anoint various families and individuals as "America's royalty." For example, the Kennedys are sometimes referred to as "America's royal family;" John F. Kennedy's presidency is commonly referred to as "Camelot," after the realm of England's mythic King Arthur. Similarly, Oprah Winfrey is often referred to as "television royalty."

Another interesting phenomena to explore is why so many Americans refer to Winfrey by her first name, as "Oprah." This continues a tradition in American TV, going back through "Arsenio" to "Dinah" and "Lucy". How does television put us on a first-name basis with people we've never met?

Caution: In order to explore this idea with your students, you may have to explore what "first-name basis" means. You could point out that school administrators are usually known by their last names, used with a title, i.e. Mr., Ms., Dr., etc. Why are people that we know in person referred to with titles, while we refer to television celebrities we've never met by their first names?

In some cultures, however, it is formal and proper to refer to people by their first names. For example, some Spanish speakers acknowledge respect and formality to refer to people as "Señor," "Señorita," "Don," "Doña" followed by the first name. In other countries, such as Indonesia, many citizens and leaders go by only a single name. Students might share the customs of their native countries regarding the appropriate use of first names.

p. 57 Search and Share

Caution : As with previous video activities, reinforce and reiterate that the video segment that students find must be in English. You can remind your students that you are aware that they already watch news, sports, soap operas and other programming in their native languages, and that they are in school to take full advantage of the class and your instruction in order to learn English. Regardless of the listening skills of your students, there will nearly always be a certain percentage of students who don't pay attention or follow directions. Reinforcement doesn't hurt.

Sound Sense: Pronunciation Practice

Or and ore have the same sound. One interesting rule in the English language is the addition of the silent "e" to words. Most English learners do not understand this, however it is to indicate a long vowel sounds versus a shorter vowel. Take a look:

	Short vowel	Long Vowel
A	Pal	Pale
I	Bill/Fill	Bile/File
E	Pet	Pete
O	Policy	Pole
U	Cut	Cute

* *More, lore, fore, tore, furthermore, therefore, bore* / Compare:

Ore ending	Rm ending
Door	Dorm
Fore	Form
More/Furthermore	Mormon
Store/tore	Storm
Swore	Swarm
War	Warm

Expansion Activities

Academic Vocabulary Expansion: Prefix/Suffix Study

Prefixes alluding to "not" or "opposite"

Contra/counter, cast, mis (mis-educate)

Contradict – To say something that is different.

Contraband – merchandise imported or exported against the law; smuggled goods

Contravene – go or act contrary to; violate; disregard; infringe

Controversy – dispute; debate; quarrel (literally 'a turning against')

Counter – contrary; in the opposite direction (followed by word TO)

Countermand – cancel (an order) by issuing a contrary order; revoke

Incontrovertible – not able to be 'turned against' or disputed; unquestionable; certain; indisputable

Phrasal Verbs

Phrasal verbs are probably the most used words in the American English language with the exception of pronouns and prepositions. The verb Get/Got are used on an hourly basis let alone daily. This is a great opportunity to review the various ways Americans use this:

I got a job	=	I found a job
I got laid off	=	I lost my job
I gotta go	=	I have to go
I gotta know	=	I have to know
I got it	=	I understand
Get a life	=	I don't like you so go away
Get even	=	I will find justice or revenge for what you did
Get away	=	I must go on a trip or vacation to relax
Get off	=	I have to leave at this station
Get married/ divorced/separated	=	To marry, divorce or separate
Gotta start	=	I must begin
Get on	=	Begin

Get over (something) – stop thinking about something.

> I can't get over the news about Sara and John. I thought they were perfect for each other.

Get away with (something) – do something wrong without punishment.

> He's not going to get away with it. The cops will catch him.

Get on with (something) – continue with something.

> Listen everyone, it's time to stop talking and get on with our class.

Get around – way to go places.

> I get around using public transportation. I don't need a car.

Get around to (something) – finally do something.

> I finally got around to doing my homework. I didn't do it for several days.

Get along with – be friendly with.

> I get along with all my classmates. They are awesome.

Get by – have enough to survive.

> I have enough money to get by until next week.

Get down to – become serious about.

> Dinner is finished and now it's time to get down to business.

Learning Objectives

➜ Students will be able to share and discuss holidays and celebrations with other students

➜ Students will be able to use common American English vocabulary regarding holidays and celebrations

➜ Students will be able to compose questions about holidays and celebrations and use them in conversations with classmates

➜ Students will be able to discuss and compose proverbs relating to holidays and celebrations

➜ Students will be able to search and share about American holidays and celebration using articles found online.

➜ Students will practice auxiliary verbs such as would and could to ask and describe hypothetical situations

➜ Students will create a calendar for holidays and special occasions and discuss them with classmates

Define and explore the meaning and origin of the word "holiday." It derives from "holy day," a day with religious significance. It is helpful to explore with your students that many holidays and the word "holiday" itself derive from religious occasions. However, it's also true that many American holidays are secular, including July 4th and Halloween. Some American holidays can be both secular and religious, like Christmas. In the United States, many secular families and even atheists celebrate the Christmas holiday as a time for families to gather and celebrate.

Minimal pair for "Date:" *Late, mate, fate, gate, hate, rate, wait, dot, dote.*

Caution: A growing number of students in recent years have announced that they will not participate in any acknowledgement, much less celebration, of the American Halloween holiday. This refusal appears to be due to a growing membership of these students in religious groups which prohibit any participation in or celebration of Halloween. Some adult school teachers have even used classroom time attempting to recruit students for membership in religious sects which oppose Halloween. It is helpful to begin by discussing the origins of each holiday. For example, the name "Halloween" derives from "Holy evening," the night before All Saint's Day in the Catholic religion. Although Halloween has origins in these Catholic customs, today most people in the United States regard it as a secular, cultural holiday.

Citizenship Connection: Explain the meaning of the term "secular" to students as meaning of any religious organization or belief. This exploration is also a good opportunity to introduce or review elements of civics and citizenship with your students: What is the highest law of the land in the United States? What guarantees our rights in this document? What are the main freedoms guaranteed by the First Amendment?

You can explain the concept of "separation of church and state" to your students, making sure that you differentiate the different definitions of these words so that students understand what this phrase means. Explain that "church" here refers not to a building but to an entire religious organization, and that "state" refers to the entire national government rather than to individual states like California and Nevada. If you are teaching in a public school, you should emphasize that you and the school are simply giving students information about important aspects of American culture, and this is not an endorsement of any particular religious organization or belief.

Depending on student populations and demographics, some adult schools also provide lessons on Ramadan, Hanukah, and Chinese New Year. These lessons do not mean the schools are endorsing any of these beliefs. You can tell your students that one of the things that makes America a great country is that we are open to people from different cultures and religions. We can combine them all into one country and one people. This forms the meaning of the national motto "e pluribus unum" on the national seal, which you can incorporate into your lesson.

If you teach at a private school, you should use your own judgment and the policies of your school as your guidelines. If any of your students balk at discussing Halloween, you can provide alternate activities, or accommodate them in other ways, depending on your own judgment and the policy of your school.

p. 62 The Conversation Continues

The Brave and the Bold: If you are adventurous and have a knack for comedy, or conversely, a stomach for more serious topics, you can explore why some people dread the holidays. How do political differences in families sometimes wreck holidays? For example, when the parents are Democrats, one child is a Republican and a cousin is a Socialist, what happens when these differences emerge in conversation at the Thanksgiving table?

You can explain and question the guideline which advises people to avoid "politics and religion" in conversation at work and social gatherings. This advice is further illustrated by the following quotes:

    ❝ The only good argument is the one you don't have."

— Dale Carnegie, American expert on interpersonal skills.

    ❝ If you can't say something nice, don't say anything at all."

— American advice

You can ask students if they think it's wise or appropriate to raise controversial issues at family gatherings. While the United States has freedom of speech and the expression, "everyone's entitled to his own opinion," perhaps other situations are more suited to controversial topics. What other situations might be more appropriate for discussing differences in religion or politics?

Another point to explore on this topic is that when these disagreements do arise, it is rare that any family member is ever able to change another family member's mind. Have you ever heard someone concede amid a gathering of other family members, "You're right? I've never thought of that." Why is that? Are people in these discussions really concerned with the issues? What other factors could be involved? Are family members sometimes in competition? Are they most concerned with their own egos? Are they really trying to convey, "I've got it all figured out." **(Explain idiom)**

Caution: Some of your students may come from countries with no freedom of speech at all, or with nominal freedom of speech "on paper," (explain idiom) but where people can be murdered when they actually speak out. Take this difference into account in your lessons and discussions.

How do all these topics compare to your students' own experiences? Cultures as diverse as Mexico, India, Italy and China highly value family structure and filial piety. How is America traditionally different? What are the pros and cons of these differences? For example, weaker family structure might offer more freedom, but less support. You can have students make lists of the advantages and disadvantages that they identify.

Another topic to explore in this area is that adult ESL students, many of whom have much stronger family ties than the average American, nonetheless undertake considerable and often permanent separation from their own families to come to America in the first place.

You can explore the students' experiences with this in writing and then move to a conversation exercise with the class or in smaller student groups. Be prepared for strong emotions and even tears to emerge as students discuss their families. These emotions do not mean this is a topic that you should avoid, but rather that it is a subject that for your students "hits them close to home." **(Explain idiom)**

To explore the most serious aspect of this topic, you can explore why some Americans become depressed and dread the holidays, and suicide rates can sometimes increase. This discussion can lead to a broader exploration of the increasing isolation of some Americans, explored in such books as "Bowling Alone" and "Living Solo." If students become distressed at this topic and express their own loneliness and anxiety about living in a foreign country, you can point out how the class itself forms a social group that is much like a family. Their school can provide a wonderful venue for finding friends and support in their new country.

The common experience of learning English as a Second Language together as adults makes students a part of a large group. Adult schools have even started families, as numerous students have met in adult school classes and then gotten married and had children. These personal relationships have even formed between students from countries as culturally and linguistically different as Mexico and France. You can point out to your students that becoming overly anxious, sad or depressed about difficult but temporary circumstances can cause them to miss or overlook social and even familial opportunities that might be right in front of them.

p. 64 Search and Share

You can give your students an additional writing assignment to describe significant holidays in their own countries, explaining why each holiday is important and what people do to celebrate. These exercises provide an excellent opportunity to give your students additional speaking experience as they explain one of their holidays to the class.

Sound Sense: Pronunciation Practice

Ame Ending	Ate Ending
Aim	Ate
Came/overcame	Crate
Fame	Fate
Game	Gate
Lame	Late
Maim	Mate/Classmate/Roomate
Tame	State

Expansion Activities

Academic Vocabulary Expansion: Prefix/Suffix Study
Prefix E for technology and the Suffix ending ous/ious.

Hyphen Words are used in English to describe the relationship between words; e-mail, e-commerce, e-learning, E-book. This is an excellent conversation starter especially as students become more and more technologically savvy and younger.

Word Form – Suffix: ous

> *ambitious, delicious, religious, dangerous, courageous, nutritious, virtuous, and suspicious.*

A valuable exercise is to have students find words that have ous suffixes and see if they recognize the words without the ous endings. Chances are the students do recognize the words.

Phrasal Verbs
Look and See

Phrasal verbs are very useful. These two verbs are also used on a daily basis and the mere addition of a preposition to them changes the entire meaning of the words.

Look after (someone or something) – 1. To take care of.
2. To make sure that someone is safe and well.

Make sure you look after your younger brother. You are in charge tonight.

I have to look after my son tonight.

Look away – To turn your eyes away from someone or something that you were looking at.

The execution of James Foley was so horrific that I had to look away.

Look for (someone or something) – 1. To search for something or someone.
2. To try and find something or someone

Can you help me look for my brother, I expected him be here 20 minutes ago.

I am looking for my black shirt. have you seen it?

Look into / Look into (something) – 1. To find out more about something in order to improve the situation.
2. To investigate or examine.

The manager promised to look into my complaint

I will look into this matter and see what I can do about it.

Look out – 1. To be careful.
2. To avoid imminent danger.

Look out for pickpockets. There are so many especially here in Times Square.

Look out! That wave is really big.

Look through – To examine something, usually quickly.

I will look through my email to see if I can find your request.

Look up – To search for information (usually in a book)

Look it up if you don't believe me. I found it on YouTube.

Look up to – To respect or admire someone.

Mark really looked up to his brother David

Chapter 10 - Being Stylish

Learning Objectives

➡ Students will be able to share views and opinions with classmates in conversations and composition

➡ Students will be able to ask and answer present and past perfect questions

➡ Students will learn common vocabulary relating to fashion and style and be able use them in conversations and composition

➡ Students will be able to compose and discuss "wh" questions regarding style and fashion

➡ Students will be able to search and share articles on the web that discuss current trends in clothing and fashion in general

➡ Students will be able outline and draft a short essay regarding a favorite article of clothing and the origins of that clothing

Students will share their essay with classmates through using presentations and visuals Explain the concepts of style and fashion to your students, some of whom may be from countries where people wear essentially the same clothes all the time. You can explore the manifestations of fashion even in situations where uniform clothing is mandated, such as uniforms in private schools and colorful headscarves in Iran. You can also explain and explore how fashion is a gigantic global industry.

Vocabulary Connection: Explaining fashion is a good opportunity to review adjectives with your students. You can show pictures or videos from various fashion shows and ask your students to describe their impressions and reactions.

You can also explore the origin and evolution of customs such as neckties and scarves. You can compare the fashions of different countries and cultures, from suits to kilts to kimonos to kaffiyehs. Students can also make spoken presentations of styles and fashions in their own countries. Are American brands or "knockoffs" (explain idiom) popular in their countries? In addition, you can explore the concept of "conformity," sometimes derided with the idiom "herd mentality." While people in some countries and cultures dress the same all the time, even people in such a seemingly individualist society such as the United States can still conform by dressing the same way as other people in a group with which they wish to be identified. In this way, wearing certain colors may be associated with a particular sports team, school, or gang.

The Brave and the Bold: If you are a more adventurous teacher, you can raise and explore the topic of how some fashions that were considered repugnant and disgusting can become mainstream (**explain idiom**). For example, two decades ago Mohawk hairstyles were restricted to the punk rock underground. They can now be seen virtually everywhere. Two decades ago, tattoos and body piercings were regarded by many as repulsive and even as a form of self-mutilation. Tattoos were traditionally associated with sailors, convicts and drug addicts. Now, tattoos and pierced noses are a common sight even among middle-aged and middle class Americans. Why are these fashions accepted now when fairly recently they were regarded as outrageous?

You can incorporate student experience into the conversation: Do you have a tattoo or more than one tattoo? Where is your tattoo? Why did you choose that design? How long did it take to put on? Did it hurt? Where did you get it put on? Why did you choose that particular venue to get your tattoo? What did you do immediately before, and immediately after, you got your tattoo? How do you feel about your tattoo now? Would you get another? Where? What does your family think of your tattoo? What kind of piercings does your culture use (e.g. some Latin American cultures pierce girls' ears shortly after birth)?

Are there any dangers to such fashion trends as tattoos and piercings? What about "buyer's remorse" **(explain idiom)**? Is there danger of hepatitis? Why do people embrace fashions that are painful, such as high heels and piercings? Is looking good (or fashionable) more important than feeling good?

❝ Why would you hang a work of art that you wouldn't hang on your wall on your body?"

— B.J. Hunnicut, a character on the television series "M.A.S.H."

❝ Tattoos don't look good on old people." — Vince Beizer, journalist

❝ I just want to be a non-conformist like everybody else."

— Robert "Shad" Northshield, television producer, quoting a friend's son

Caution: As always, use your judgment in these discussion. Tattoos and piercings straddle an unusual intersection of the public and the private. On the one hand, as they are etched on the skin, they are very public, and meant for display and discussion. On the other hand, it is possible that students may become defensive if they feel that they are being somehow criticized for their tattoos or piercings. It is best to keep a spirit and tone of open-minded inquiry, and you will nearly always find that your students are quite willing to discuss their more extreme fashion choices.

p. 69 The Conversation Continues

To extend the conversation, you can ask students what they like most about American clothes and fashion compared with those in their native country. Additionally, what do they dislike most? Be prepared for a wide array of answers. Some students might think American clothing is too revealing, while others might think that American clothes are too constricting and uncomfortable.

Minimal pair for "Style:" *Tile, pile, dial, mile, guile, Nile, while, smile, stall, stale, steel, stole, stool.*

p. 71 Search and Share

You can bring in fashion magazines, or have your students bring in their own material. If they bring their own native fashion magazines, this gives the students additional opportunities to explain this material in English. You may be amazed at what you discover. For example, one student from Mongolia had a picture of a popular Mongolian music group dressed in regalia resembling Genghis Khan. The student explained that Genghis Khan is a national hero in Mongolia, and that in Mongolia Genghis Khan costumes and hats never go out of style!

Sound Sense: Pronunciation Practice

Ot Ending	Ole Ending
Bot/Robot	Bole
Cot	Coal
Got	Goal
Hot	Hole
Pot	Pole
Rot	Role

Hint: use body language to describe the difference of the sole of your shoe as opposed to your soul (pointing to your heart).

Expansion Activities

Academic Vocabulary Expansion: Prefix/Suffix Study
Suffixes for languages, culture and religion

Word Form: *Ish, ese, an, i.*

This fun and informative exercise allows students to go around the class and ask their classmates where they are from and what nationality, language, and other cultural aspects they have experienced. You can show how different languages, nationalities and ethnicities have different, yet common suffix endings.

    ESE – Chinese, Japanese, Vietnamese, Congolese, Taiwanese, Lebanese, Portuguese, etc.

    AN – Korean, Ghanaian, Ugandan, Libyan, Argentinian, Brazilian, Chilean (All of Latin America) Norwegian, Saudi Arabian.

    ISH – British, Scottish, Irish, Finnish, Danish, Swedish, Kurdish, Spanish.

    I – Iraqi, Israeli, Sunni, Ismailia, Swahili, Hindi, Pakistani, Farsi.

Phrasal Verbs
Work

Phrasal verbs with the word work can be challenging and fun at the same time. In this lesson emphasize that certain phrasal verbs are separable while other are inseparable. For example, work out is separable (Work something out) while work around is not.

To work around (something) – to find a way of organizing an activity avoiding any problems.

> The deadlines are very short, but I'm sure you can find a way to work around them.

To work off – to overcome the effects of something by doing something energetic or different.

> We should hit the gym and work off the pizza we had for dinner.

To work on (something) – to spend time and effort trying to perfect it.

> In training, he's been working on improving the weak parts of his game.

To work out (1) – to calculate the solution to a mathematical problem.

> I've tried working this problem out several times. Yet I still can't figure it out.

To work out (2) – to think carefully to find a solution to a problem.

> Nobody has worked out a solution to this problem. We are still spending too much.

To work out (3) – to do physical exercise to improve your fitness.

> She works out every other day. No wonder she is in such great shape.

Chapter 11 - Handling Stress

Learning Objectives

➡ Students will be able to share tips about coping with stress with fellow classmates

➡ Students will learn prefixes meaning "not" such as un, il, ir, im, non and dis.

➡ Students will be able to write questions using the vocabulary in the chapter and practice asking and answering questions with classmates

➡ Students will be able to search and share tips to reducing stress using internet search skills

➡ Students will take a five minute stress test online and report back to class their findings and opinions about the test

Students will be able to write a short entry in the book about an event in their life them to be stressed and share with the class

Explain the concept of stress as it is defined in American culture. You may be surprised to discover that some of your students are unfamiliar with this term in the sense that Americans use it. Explain that while stress is a noun, it also has an idiomatic use as a verb, as in "I'm really stressed at work right now." A good way to start with this topic is with a reading lesson using an article about reducing stress. These articles will usually explain the origin of the modern American idea of "stress" to the biological "fight or flight" response, which goes back to the origins of human beings as cave people and hunter gatherers.

Although we have now developed modern civilization, the biological imperatives of our primitive ancestors remain with us. However, they are not necessarily productive in modern life. A worker cannot pick up a heavy rock and smash his boss over the head when feeling overly pressured. Thus, in the modern United States we have the ideas of "stress management:" dealing with and reducing stress.

Having established and defined the concept of stress, you can further introduce and develop the concept by asking students what sort of events can be stressful, and what has been stressful for them in their lives, from supporting a family to taking care of parents to raising children.

    " People who want to do everything all at once generally don't get anything done."

—Jerry Brown, Governor of California

Grammar Connection: This chapter offers a good opportunity to review auxiliary verbs such as "Can" (what situations can be stressful?) and the present perfect tense. (When have you felt stress in your life? Have you ever had a level of stress that you felt you couldn't handle? What was the reason?)

p. 74 Expanding Vocabulary

For life as a "roller coaster" (explain idiom) you can bring in pictures or even toys to illustrate what a roller coaster is. Many of your students may be unfamiliar with amusement parks. Depending on your school's own geographic proximity to amusement parks, you can use local examples, i.e. amusement parks that are within driving distance of your school. If you are too far from any such amusement parks, you can show pictures and discuss world-famous establishments like Disneyland and Six Flags. You can reinforce the present perfect (see Grammar Connection above) by asking students "Have you ever been on a roller coaster," "Would you like to go on a roller coaster?" etc.

Minimal pair for "Cope:"
Cap, cape, cup, cop, mope, hope, rope, dope, lope, grope, pope.

Ap Ending	Op Ending	Up Ending	Ope Ending
Cap	Cop	Cup	Cope
Happy	Hop	Brushup	Hope
Map	Mop	Muppet	Mope
Rap	Drop	Rupture	Rope

p. 76 The Conversation Continues

You can explore with your students the negative health effects of stress. You can also explore the consequences of some of the bad habits people develop to manage stress, such as smoking and drinking. What are some more healthy habits that people can use to manage stress (e.g. exercise or meditation)? How do religious beliefs help people manage stress (e.g. meditation, yoga, the Old Testament advisory that "This too shall pass")?

p. 76-77 Discussing Quotations

You can explore the Jung quotation with your students by introducing the idea that all drama is based on conflict. Overcoming obstacles is difficult, by definition, but it is the source of all accomplishment, satisfaction and self-esteem. Ask your students to imagine a world with no conflict or problems. Life might be very easy, but also extremely dull. You can also introduce and discuss the strange human tendency and desire to cause problems where none are present, from the local neighborhood gossip to schoolyard bullies to expansionist military dictators.

p. 78 Search and Share

You can pair or otherwise group students to make lists of things that cause stress and things that reduce stress. You can also have them make lists of good habits to reduce stress and bad habits to reduce stress.

Sound Sense: Pronunciation Practice

Teach the short and long e vowel sounds. Make sure to mention how the double ee (as when we say "cheese" using the mouth muscles more than the short vowel.

> *See, sea, plea, be, bee, fee, flea, flee, free, he, knee, me, she, ski, tea, tee, three, we.*

More difficult one:

> *Spree, agree, carefree, degree, sightsee, guarantee, refugee, referee.*

Compare those to those ending with a "d" sound.

> *Freed, kneed, reed, seed, speed, read.*

More difficult one:

> *Greed, concede, exceed, force-feed, precede, proceed, guaranteed, supersede.*

Expansion Activities

Academic Vocabulary Expansion: Prefix/Suffix Study
Prefix Co/com: meaning together.

These common prefixes demonstrate the meaning of "together."

Examples:
Combination, coexist, conspiracy, co-educational (or Coed for short), cooperate, coordinate, compile, competition, community, compatible.

Phrasal Verbs

To talk about – Very popular expression meaning simply to discuss a topic

> Hey, good thing you came. We were just talking about you.

To talk back – means to reply rudely instead of being polite.

> He was very polite and didn't talk back to his parents.

To talk down – Means to reduce the importance of something, make something smaller than it is.

> They talked down the success of our project as they were very jealous.

To talk down to – Means someone is peaking to someone as if they were inferior to you.

> She talked down to me as if I was a child.

To talk someone into – Means to persuade someone to do something.

> He doesn't want to do it but I think I can talk him into it.

To talk someone out of – Means to persuade someone not to do something.

> I talked her out of buying that car. She doesn't need to spend so much money.

To talk over – Means to discuss a problem or situation before making a decision.

> Can we talk it over? I think you are being too hasty.

Chapter 12 - Practicing Job Interviews

Learning Objectives

→ Students will be able to practice and simulate job interviews

→ Students will review key interview questions and practice answering them in class with their teachers and classmates

→ Students will learn and practice using key job and interview vocabulary

→ Students will compare and contrast jobs experiences from their countries and the United States

→ Students will learn and discuss basic work etiquette in the United States

→ Students will search and share videos online concerning advice on job interview techniques

→ Students will be asked to give feedback on the videos they watched specifically for the efficacy of the advice in the videos

→ Students will make a list of steps to take in hiring new employees then share their tips with the class

You can warm-up and review for this chapter by asking how many students have a job. Ask how people get jobs in the United States. Finding work is not always an easy thing, particularly in an uncertain economy. You can define and explain the concepts of patronage and nepotism. However, most people in America have had to apply and interview to get their jobs. You can explore how this is an aspect of America as a free country; many students may be from countries where people are employed through families, political parties or the government.

You can also do a tie-in lesson of how American workplaces are structured. Explain the different meanings and roles of a foreman, supervisor, manager and owner.

Minimal pair for "Think:" *Thing, thin, thank, link, sink, blink, brink, wink, fink, mink, rink, pink.*

p. 83 The Conversation Continues

You can expand the conversation by adding these quotations to the mix:

" If you're not getting better, you're getting worse."

— American saying

" God helps those who help themselves."

— American saying

" People rise to their own level of incompetence"

— the Peter Principle of Dr. Laurence J. Peter

Explain to your students the concept of skill. Define and explain the meaning of the word professional as meaning that you are paid to do something. It does not necessarily mean that you are good at it. For example, some professional entertainers and comedians may not be that entertaining to many people, but they are still considered professional because they are paid to perform.

You can pair or otherwise group students to make lists of skills they have and skills they would like to improve. For example, reading, writing and speaking their native language are skills they already have. Reading, writing and speaking English are skills they want to improve. That, of course, is why they are in your class. You can incorporate sayings and quotes like those above or others that you may find to introduce and explore the importance of maintaining, developing and expanding skills in a competitive modern economy.

Sound Sense: Pronunciation Practice

Hop, shop, top, mop, cop, slop, stop, chop, crop, drop, flop, prop.

More difficult words:

Eavesdrop, doorstop, pawnshop, hip hop, rain drop, rooftop, short stop, workshop, mountain top

Compare them to the long o ending:

Cope, scope, soap, mope, nope.

More difficult words:

Elope, slope, envelope, horoscope, microscope, stethoscope, tightrope.

Expansion Activities

Academic Vocabulary Expansion: Prefix/Suffix Study
Prefix Pro/Anti

The prefixes for pro and con can be easily explained as their stand-alone meaning: Pro and con. A fun activity would be to compare opposites while using pro and con. However, it is important to note that not all have direct opposites. In fact, pro also means forward or to elevate. Pro with many nouns simply means in favor of.

Popular words: *Pro-democracy, pro-choice and pro-life, anti-communist, anti-Semite, anti-aircraft, antagonist and protagonist.*

Phrasal Verbs

Fall and Fill

We like teaching the phrasal verbs for "fill" because they can be confusing for students. Everyone will need to know those common phrasal verbs eventually.

Take for example these two sentences:

> Fill out this form and return it to the front office please.

> Please fill in the following information about yourself and return it to the front office.

Although these sentences are similar, there are always nuances in the English language that must be explained to students. Fill out a form could indicate that an important form such as a job or DMV application must filled out to its entirety. Fill in could refer to a less complicated form that only requires basic information about yourself such as a doctor's visit or a store survey.

Chapter 13 - Valuing Money and Finding Bargains

Learning Objectives

→ Students will share experiences about personal finances

→ Students will learn and be able to use vocabulary relating to money and budgeting

→ Students will be able to distinguish between prepositions used in prepositional phrases

→ Students will learn and be able to use customer services sentences and vocabulary

→ Students will practice customer service scenarios both as customers and service personnel

→ Students will be able to write consumer complaint and response sentences using prepositional phrases

→ Students will be able to search and share online information concerning estimated budgets and living expenses in different geographical areas of the United States

→ Students will share consumer behaviors in their countries with classmates

You can introduce a discussion of money by actually showing and discussing money. Another way to warm up, review and introduce this topic is to ask students what they like to do in their free time. Shopping, movies, travel, parties? You can then ask what is necessary to do all of these things: money.

Vocabulary Connection - This chapter provides a good time and opportunity to review the names and denominations of American money. Even advanced students may be recent arrivals who are less familiar with American money then you might think. This monetary overview can also be expanded to a lesson which gives students speaking practice by showing and explaining the different bills and denominations of money from their native countries.

You can also explain and explore the idea of exchange rates. Why are some currencies worth more than others? Why do so many people and countries prefer to keep their money in dollars, followed in popularity by Euros and Pounds Sterling? Why do some countries choose "dollarization," which is to abandon their own currencies and use American dollars? El Salvador, for example, recently dropped colones in favor of dollars, and Zimbabwe replaced its own astronomically inflating currency with American dollars.

p. 88 Paraphrasing Proverbs

Some additional proverbs include:

> No money, no honey   — American

> Money talks, nonsense walks   — American

Caution: Students will sometimes bring in the above and other expressions that are commonly used with profanity. Depending on the demographic of your class, the rules of your school, and your own temperament, you can allude or explain that variations of expressions such as the one above often are expressed with profanity. You can further explain that you are not going to describe these expressions with profanity as that is not appropriate for your classroom environment.

You can likewise suggest to your students that profanity is not appropriate for them to use in the workplace and most social environments. Students may respond that their supervisors, co-workers and others use copious profanity in the workplace, to which you might respond that it is still not generally acceptable.

p. 90 The Conversation Continues

You can discuss different uses of money. You can also discuss and have students list good and bad habits with money. Good habits might include saving, spending within means, and paying off bills and debts. Bad habits might include living paycheck to paycheck (explain idiom), overspending, and allowing bills and debts to accumulate.

Practicing Prepositions - p. 90 - Emphasize to your students the American motto, "Practice makes perfect." As prepositions don't always follow intuitive or regular patterns, one of the best tools for mastering prepositions is to simply listen for their usage and practice with them as much as possible. With patience and persistence, prepositions will become easier.

Minimal Pair for "Tip:" *Tap, tape, type, top, rip, skip, hip, lip, nip, pip, sip, zip, whip.*

Technology Connection p. 90:
You can expand the conversation by bringing in the element of handling banking, credit card transactions, tax returns and other financial matters over the internet: Do you use the internet to handle financial business? Why or why not? What are some advantages of using the internet? (speed, accessibility, ease of use) What are some disadvantages? (hacking, security)

p. 92-93 Discussing Quotations

You can expand the conversation by throwing the following quotation into the mix:

" I've been rich and I've been poor. Rich is better"

— Beatrice Kaufman (1895-1945) American writer

You can discuss these quotations with questions: Are Americans too preoccupied with money? The common American for this is that people can be too "materialistic." This meaning is very different from the philosophical, political or religious meanings of the word "materialism." What are the things that money can't buy? Some examples might include family, true friendship, and love.

p. 94 Search and Share

Explain and explore the very American concept and expression "the cost of living." You can pair or otherwise group students to list the various items that make up the cost of living: housing (rent or mortgage), food, clothes, water, electricity, phone, cell phone, children, etc. Is the cost of living higher in the United States or in your home country? Why does the cost of living vary among American cities and states? Why is the cost of living higher in cities like Los Angeles, San Francisco and New York? Why is the cost of living lower in smaller cities and rural areas?

Sound Sense: Pronunciation Practice

In Ending	Ine Ending	More Challenging
Berlin	Line	Airline/Sunshine
Bin	Bind	Combine
Dinner	Dine	
Fin	Fine	Confine
Pin	Pine	Opine
Sin	Sign	Design
Spin	Spine	
Win	Wine	Whine

Even more advanced students:

Cosign, align, assign, coastline, confine, decline, define, guideline, grapevine, hotline, outline, recline, refine, resign.

You could also compare it to "ink"

Ink, blink, drink, link, pink, shrink, sink, think, wink.

For more advanced students:

Zinc, hoodwink, clink, rethink, soft drink, rethink.

Expansion Activities

Academic Vocabulary Expansion: Prefix/Suffix Study
Prefixes Mid, trans, sub

The prefix mid is found in everyday words such as midnight, midmorning midterm. Although your students already know these, have them focus on more difficult words from all aspects of English for Specific Purposes. For example, in medical English students learn about the midsection of the body and midwives while they might have to know transplant, and transfusion. In business English they would learn about substandard, subdivision, transaction, transnational and midpoint of delivery.

Phrasal Verbs

Pay for, pay up, payback, paying attention, etc.

To make the class more interesting, make up a quiz prior to the class and have students test their knowledge either alone or in groups (groups are preferred for conversational purposes). Hers is a way to take the verb "pay" and have students figure out (another great phrasal verb) which prepositions are the right one and the meaning of the sentence without the teacher's help.

1) She never paid _____ the money she had borrowed from them

       over

       back

       against

2) When you deposit money in your bank account, you pay_____

       in

       off

       to

3) She paid _____ full at the end of the night, so it didn't cost us a penny

out

in

for

4) Jack the Ripper was never caught and didn't pay _____ his crimes

back

for

in

5) She paid fifty dollars _____ her savings account yesterday

onto

into

at

6) She paid _____ the dinner

into

onto

for

7) I want revenge- I'm going to pay him _____ for that insult. It's pay .....time!

back

over

into

8) Criminals should pay _____ their crimes

       for

       from

       by

9) The workers were paid _____ when they were made redundant

       out

       off

       in

10) She had to ask him several times for the money he owed her before he finally paid _____

       to

       into

       up

Learning Objectives

→ Students will learn about American cities and discuss similarities and differences between them and those found in other countries

→ Students will be able to share their experiences traveling to American cities with classmates

→ Students will learn and be able to use vocabulary relating to urban living

→ Students will write about major landmarks in their favorite city and share with the class

→ Students will discuss transportation systems in America and their countries

→ Students will be able to write and share experiences in different cities using adjectives and sentences of description

Students will be able to search and share an article concerning an American city
You can warm up, review and introduce this topic by first giving the students exercises to talk about their own backgrounds. Are you from a small town or a big city? Is Tokyo a small town or a big city? How about Mexico City? You can create elaborate comprehension checks with specific questions about where your students are from, whether it is Bretagne, France or Cojutepeque, El Salvador.

You can expand this warm-up exercise by pairing or otherwise grouping students to make lists of the advantages and disadvantages (pros and cons) (explain idiom) of small towns and big cities. Small towns might yield you pros of more living space, friendly neighbors, and a cheaper cost of living. Cons might include provincialism, limited medical care, and limited cultural attractions. Big cities might offer pros of excitement, nightlife, cosmopolitan environment, diversity and cultural attractions. Cons could be crime, noise, traffic and isolation from neighbors.

You can bring in posters, postcards and slide projections from the internet or your own photos to illustrate the cities discussed for the students. Encourage students to bring in their own materials from their own vacations and travels.

p. 99 - 100 Discussing Quotations

Find some quotes on the internet or in your own reading and experience about the city or area where you live. Here, for example, are some classic quotes about Los Angeles, the city of origin for Compelling American Conversations:

❝ The only culture in Los Angeles is in the yogurt.” — Popular joke

❝ Tip the world over on its side and everything loose will land in Los Angeles.”

— Frank Lloyd Wright

❝ I could hear everything, together with the hum of my hotel neon. I never felt sadder in my life. LA is the loneliest and most brutal of American cities; NY gets god-awful cold in the winter, but there's a feeling of wacky comradeship somewhere in some streets. LA is a jungle.”

— Jack Kerouac, On the Road- Jack Kerouac, Writer

❝ It's [Los Angeles] mostly full of nonsense and delusion and egomania. They think they'll be young and beautiful forever, even though most of them aren't even young and beautiful now."

— Christopher Hitchens, writer

❝ I don't want to live in a place where the only cultural advantage is the ability to turn right on a red light."

— Woody Allen in *Annie Hall*

p. 101 Search and Share

You can use a variation of this activity where students find an article about their hometown or a major city in their own home country and present it to the class. The article must be in English - either written in English, or, depending on the ambition and level of your students, they can pick articles in their native language and translate them into English before presenting them to the class. The same questions apply: What do you like about this city? Why is it important in your country? Why is it important to the world? Some of the answers may surprise you. For example, Michoacan, Mexico, is one of the largest exporters of avocados in the world. In recent years, their biggest customer in the global avocado market has been...China! You can use global economic and cultural connections like this to explore and enhance social interaction and cohesion in your class among students of many diverse national origins.

Sound Sense: Pronunciation Practice

A good practice for this chapter will be the ip vs. ap endings.

Ip Ending	AP Ending
Chip	Chap
Clip	Clap
Flip	Flap
Hip	Happen
Lip	Lap
Nip	Nap
Sip	Sap
Slip	Slap
Tip	Tap

For the more advanced students:

Quip, blip, catnip, courtship, friendship, hardship, spaceship, censorship, fellowship, internship, leadership, membership, scholarship, championship, citizenship.

Chap, lap, clap, cap, flap, gap, nap, rap, scrap, slap, snap, tap, trap, zap, wrap.

For even more advanced students:

Road map, unwrap, handicap, black slap, gift wrap, mishap, recap, fire trap, bottle cap, wiretap.

Expansion Activities

Academic Vocabulary Expansion: Prefix/Suffix Study
Prefix: re, circum

The prefixes of re, meaning again, and circum meaning around.

Recharge, review, rebuttal, reinvent, recycle.

Circumspect, circumnavigate, circumstance, circumlocution are good examples.

Phrasal Verbs

Try out – Means to test or experiment with

>   The city of Los Angeles is trying out the new bike lanes they built throughout the city.

>   Google is trying out its new "google glass" to see if it's working properly

Try out – Means to try to get on a team

>   Danny is trying out for the high school soccer team this fall. I hope he makes it.

Try on – To see if something fits

>   Vivian tried on her new bikini just in time for the summer season.

Chapter 15 - Seeing our World with Photographs

Learning Objectives

→ Students will be able to share lasting memories regarding events in their lives

→ Students will choose a photograph and describe it with classmates

→ Students will be able to share their opinions and thoughts

→ Students will choose photographs and write captions regarding the photographs

→ Students will practice conditional sentences using the "if" clauses by asking and answering if questions

→ Students will be able to search and share important moments in time using historical photographs

→ Students will be able to write a descriptive essay about a favorite photograph and discuss it with the class

You can introduce this chapter by asking how many of your students own cameras. Do they prefer digital or film cameras? Or do they take all their pictures on their cell phone? Younger students will probably never have known anything but digital photography. Older students may still be making the transition to new digital photography technology, and some may even still be shooting on film.

You can work these concerns into the conversation with questions: When did photography change from being exclusively on film to primarily digital? Why did people make this change? What is convenient about shooting on digital? What are the inconveniences of shooting on film? Why do many professional photographers even today prefer to shoot on film? (answer: many photographers think that film still offers a much better spectrum of colors than digital. Highlights, or areas of more intense light, such as skies and windows, can also appear "blown out" or washed out, in digital photography.

p. 106 The Conversation Continues

Make sure your students understand the concepts and definitions of terms such as "paparazzi." A tragic if illustrative example of the phenomena would be the death of Princess Diana while being pursued by photographers on motorcycles. Other examples include famous actors such as Sean Penn spending time in jail for assaulting photographers.

Photo Family: Have your students bring in their favorite photos of their families and friends, or perhaps trips they have taken, or any other photo subjects that fit in with your class. You can model this activity by showing and explaining some of your own photographs to students.

Minimal pair for "Click:" *Clock, cloak, chick, sick, pick, nick, tick, wick, hick, quick.*

Photo Fun: Using one or more of the photographs below, pair or otherwise group students and have them guess the profession, background and other characteristics of the person in the photo.

p. 106-107 Discussing Quotations

"Being a photographer is like having Christmas every day."

— Bruce Weber, photographer.

You can discuss with your students what Weber means by this. Once they give their answers, you can tell them that the interview with Weber was conducted before the advent of digital cameras, when all photographers shot on film with analog cameras. Weber was talking about being able to open the packages he got from the film labs to see how his photos turned out.

Sound Sense: Pronunciation Practice

Um Sound Ending	Un Sound Ending	Ump Sound Ending
Bum	Bun	Bump
Dumb	Done	Dump
Gum	Gun	Gump
Rum	Run	Rump
Slum	Slung	Slump
Stun	Stumble	Stump

For more advanced students:

Broad jump, city dump, ski jump, goose bump, speed bump, stomach pump.

Expansion Activities

Academic Vocabulary Expansion: Prefix/Suffix Study
Prefix: Il, Ir, Im
Suffix: hood, dom

The Prefixes for Il, ir, im all refer to not. Il normally precedes a word with an l, ir with r and im with a p.

> *Illegal, illegitimate, illegible, illogical.*
>
> *Irresponsible, irregular, irrational, irresistible.*
>
> *Impossible, implausible, impassible, impotent, impaired.*

Phrasal Verbs

Fall off/apart/through/out

Fall off – To disappear or literally fall off of something.

> What happened to Jimmy? It's as if he fell off the face of the earth.

Fall apart – To lose yourself, to despair.

> Jordan fell apart after his wife left him. He really loved her.

Fall through – An expression usually meaning that something did not work out. It can also be used with fall through the cracks.

> What happened to that deal you had to launch a new school? It fell through when the main investor decided to pull out (another great phrasal verb meaning withdraw).

Fall out – Become detached and drop out

> John doesn't talk to his in-laws these days. They had a falling out over money issues.

Appendix

Reproducible Exercises   92

Quotes and Proverbs Worksheets   95

Adding Your Voice to Class Discussions   97

Hedging Language   99

Tips to Becoming More Active   102
in Classroom Discussions

Some Media Suggestions   104

REPRODUCIBLE EXERCISES

Lesson Plans

Topic:	Date:
# of Participants:	Room:
# of Groups:	Pages:

Give Opening Quote:

_____

_____

Make brief opening comment to class:

_____

_____

Select three questions to introduce the topic:

1. _____

_____

2. _____

_____

3. _____

_____

Review Vocabulary:

- Expand vocabulary for class discussion (5-10 minutes)

- List new words that could be used for academic discussion

Pair Students off for conversation (Record starting time):

- Allow 20-40 minutes for conversation

- Circulate among students and take notes

Conversation Content:

What did you hear the students say?

```
┌─────────────────────────────────────────────────────────────────┐
│ Summarize:                                                        │
│                                                                   │
│                                                                   │
│                                                                   │
│                                                                   │
│                                                                   │
│                                                                   │
│                                                                   │
└─────────────────────────────────────────────────────────────────┘
```

Select three class discussion questions (Prepare to lead 20 minutes class discussion):

1. _____

_____

2. _____

_____

3. _____

_____

Lead Class Discussion:

- Lead 20-30 minutes discussion

- Call on wide range of students

Provide Pronunciation tips:

- Review overhead "good mistakes" (10 minutes)

- Model proper pronunciation, review sound patterns

- Find a minimal pair to contrast

Note Grammar Issues:

- Review "good mistakes" and grammar notes

Good Mistakes:	Grammar Notes:

Provide other comments/observations:

Comments:	Observations:

Summarize Class Lesson:

- Thank Students for sharing insights and making "good mistakes"

- Ask students to write one question and find one proverb/question related to the next chapter.

Additional Observations:

_____

_____

_____

_____

_____

_____

QUOTES AND PROVERBS WORKSHEETS

Pronunciation Points:

List below the words that you found difficult to pronounce. Break the word down into syllables (Example: Poet = Po/et, Compromise = Com/pro/mise, Disagreeable = Dis/agree/able). Then read each syllable slowly, increasing speed once you are more comfortable with each syllable. In the case of the word "Disagreeable" you will also find syllables help understand prefixes, roots and suffixes. For further practice, break down the word even further and try to see if the letter is voiced/voiceless.

Word	Syllables	Voiced/Voiceless

Punctuation Points to Consider:
(Please make notes for each question. This will help you understand the quote/proverb better)

For Each quote/proverb you choose, highlight and list below (if any) the punctuation used.

Examples, *colon, comma, semi colon, exclamation point, etc.*
Punctuation is important in understanding the writer's intent, nuances and main point. Do a quick internet search to find more meaning and tie together the use of punctuation with the quote/proverb you learned.

1. _____
_____
2. _____
_____
3. _____
_____
4. _____
_____
5. _____
_____

Grammar Points to Consider:
(Please make notes for each question. This will help you understand the quote/proverb better)

For Each quote/proverb you choose, highlight and list below (if any) the grammar used.

Examples, *simple/compound/complex sentences, clauses, etc.*
Grammar is also very important in understanding the writer's intent, nuances and main point. Do a quick internet search to find meaning and tie together the use of grammar with the quote/proverb.

1. _____
   _____
2. _____
   _____
3. _____
   _____
4. _____
   _____
5. _____
   _____

Adding Your Voice to Class Discussions

What are three barriers to integration into classroom discussions?

-
-
-

What are three common misperceptions about your country and culture? What should your American classmates know that they do not know about your country or culture?

-
-
-

If a fellow college student from another country visited your city/region/country, what would you want to share with this international visitor/tourist? Why?

-
-
-

What are three important events in your native nation's history? Why are these events important and significant?

-
-
-

Let's travel back a bit in time. What were some important public policy issues, concerns, debates, or problems in the following years? (If you don't know the exact year, consider the surrounding five year period.)

2014:

1964:

1914

What are three important values for you? Can you give an example to support each value?

1.

2.

3.

Hedging Language

Name – Can you share a favorite slogan or proverb?

1.

2.

3.

4.

5.

6.

7.

8.

9.

10.

11.

12.

13.

14.

66 Education is a kind of continuing dialogue and a dialogue assumes, in the nature of the case, different points of view."

— Robert Hutchins (1899-1977), educator and philosopher

Hedging Language: Poetry vs Accuracy

What are three vague generalizations about the United States?

-
-
-

What are some proverbs or slogans from your country or culture?

-
-
-

What are some popular songs that make universal claims?

-
-

Can you think of two sayings that contradict each other?

-
-

Techniques for turning vague generalizations with more accurate, responsible statements:

- Add frequency adverb (sometimes, seldom, often)

- Weaken the verb (seem to, appear, tend to)

- Add modal (can, may, might,)

- Add qualifier (one of the best, an effective method)

- Identify conditions (when the information is known)

- Cite source (according to a 2013 WHO report)

Can you rewrite a generalization about USC or Los Angeles?

-

Can you rephrase a traditional proverb or popular slogan?

-

Seek Clarification: Key phrases

Checking what someone means:

> What do you mean by that?
> Do you mean...?
> In other word....?
> So are you saying...?
> Can you clarify that statement?
> Correct me if I'm wrong, but do you mean...?
> Sorry, I'm not sure if I got that. Are you saying...?
> Asking someone to explain what they mean:
> Could you expand on that?
> Which means what?
> Which means exactly what? (more sceptical)
> What are the implications?
> Can you spin that out?
> Sorry, what exactly do you mean by that?
> Sorry, could you go over that again?

Checking that someone has understood you:

> Is that clear?
> Are you with me?
> Does that make everything clear?
> Can we move on?

66 The corruption of man is followed by the corruption of language."

— Ralph Waldo Emerson American writer and philosopher

Tips to Becoming More Active in Classroom Discussions

Do the homework: Come prepared

- prepare questions

- find a relevant, recent media story

Ask questions

1. Admit you don't know

    - And be curious!

2. Seek clarification

    - What do you mean?

    - Can you clarify a bit more?

    - In other words, you are saying....

    - Can you spin that out for me?

3. Be sceptical – and tactful

    - Ask for additional details, examples

    - Says who? Seek sources

    - Are you sure? How sure are you?

4. Express your opinon (and ambivalence is okay)

    - Use Hedging language

    - On one hand....

    - It seems/appears/looks like/feels like

5.   Demonstrate how many problems remain complicated

- Consider diverse perspectives

- Look at stakeholders

- Consider technology

- Help move beyond the "obvious" into the subtle

6.   Share Evidence (It's okay to disagree – even with the professor!)

- Bring new information (experience: personal, national) to the table

- Do we know.....

- Is it possible....

- What if you are wrong?

7.   Become who you are

- Don't forget what you bring to table

- Culture counts

8.   Speculate

- I wonder .... I wonder if .... I wonder how .... I wonder who

- Help your college class become a truly global classroom

"We learn by doing." — English Proverb

Some Media Suggestions:

Radio:

BBC Radio

Voice of America

TED Radio Hour

Science Fridays

Marketplace Radio

Print Media:

The Daily Trojan

The L.A. Times

USA Today

The Wall Street Journal

The New York Times

The Economist

Time Magazine

Websites for Insights/Stories on American Culture:

Storycorps.org   ThisIbelieve.org

TED.com   ThisAmericanLife.org

Snapjudgement.org   Themoth.org

COMPELLING AMERICAN CONVERSATIONS

REPRODUCIBLE SEARCH AND SHARE COLLECTION

Written and Edited by
Eric H. Roth
HalBogotch
Toni Aberson

[REPRODUCIBLE]

SEARCH and SHARE

Watching the News

Student Name: .... Date: ....

Class: .... Teacher: ....

"Search and Share" exercises ask you to find information on your own and bring the information back to your classmates to discuss in small groups. This homework exercise helps you use real English materials, and bring your voice into the classroom.

For homework, watch a news report in your best language for 5-10 minutes. You can use the TV or the Internet to find a video in which a news announcer is sitting in the studio presenting the news.

First watch the news with the sound "muted," or with the volume turned all the way down, so you can focus on the presenter's body language. As you watch, look at the speaker's face (especially on his or her mouth) and on the speaker's hand and body movements.

Video (non-English): ....

Source: .... Topic: ....

Captions or descriptions: ....

Next, find another 5-10 minute news report on TV or on the Internet in English. Like before, watch it with the volume as low as possible or on the "mute" setting. While you watch, again pay close attention to the person's mouth, face, hands, and gestures.

Video (English): ....

Source: .... Topic: ....

Captions or descriptions: ....

Here are a few places to search for news videos: **http://www.youtube.com/education** and **hulu.com**.

Describe the person speaking your best language.

Describe the person speaking English.

Was the mouth of either announcer open wide more often?

What did you notice about the person's face or hands?

What else did you see?

What do you think this means? Why?

[REPRODUCIBLE]

SEARCH and SHARE

We're Talking About My Hometown!

Student Name: .... Date: ....

Class: .... Teacher: ....

All people are shaped by the place where they were born or grew up. Where were you born? What would you like to tell us about your hometown?

Please find a story on the Internet (in English) about your hometown or native land that you would like to share with your classmates. Read the article, print it out, and be prepared to discuss it.

Title: ....

Author: .... Length: ....

Publication: .... Publication date: ....

What's the main idea?

How many sources were quoted?

Were there any photos or illustrations? What kind?

What did you learn from this article?

What was the most interesting part for you?

Write five new vocabulary words, idioms, or expressions related to the article.

    1.

    2.

    3.

    4.

    5.

How would you rate the article, on a scale of 1–5, with five being the highest? Why?

Why did you choose this article?

> **"Light tomorrow with today!"**
> —*Elizabeth Barrett Browning (1806-1861), British poet*

[REPRODUCIBLE]

SEARCH and SHARE

Finding English Pronunciation Tips on YouTube!

Student Name: .... Date: ....

Class: .... Teacher: ....

Find a YouTube (or Hulu.com) video clip that gives tips or suggestions on improving English pronunciation. Look for better ways to make certain sounds (example: the consonant blend, 'str' as in strong). You can also search for common word stress patterns in English. Watch the video, listen carefully, take notes, and share the pronunciation tips with your classmates.

Video title: ....

Web address: ....

Length: ....   Creator: ....

Describe the video. Who is the presenter? What happens?

What pronunciation tips did the video give?

Which words or sounds did the video focus on?

What was the strongest part? Why?

What was the weakest part? Why? What would you add?

Who do you think would be the best audience for this video?

What did you learn from this video?

Why did you choose this video?

How would you rate this video, on a scale of 1–5, with five being the highest? Why?

> **"Fatherhood is helping your children learn English as a foreign language."**
> —*Bill Cosby (1937–), American comedian and actor*

SEARCH and SHARE

Always Be Yourself

Student Name: .... Date: ....

Class: .... Teacher: ....

Please find a video about being yourself on **Hulu.com** or **YouTube.com**.

What is the segment about?

Can you describe one or two of the characters?

Did the main character face a problem? What was it?

What was the main idea of this video?

What was the most interesting part for you? Why?

Write five new vocabulary words, idioms, or expressions related to the topic.

    1.

    2.

    3.

    4.

    5.

Do you think "being yourself" is always a good idea? Why? Why not?

How would you rate the video on a scale of 1–5, with five being the highest? Why?

> **"This above all: to thine own self be true."**
>
> —*William Shakespeare (1564–1616), English playwright*

[REPRODUCIBLE]

SEARCH and SHARE

Chatting: In Person or Online

Student Name: .... Date: ....

Class: .... Teacher: ....

Find an article about how friendship has changed since Facebook, Google+, and Twitter have become so popular.

Read the article, print it out, and be prepared to discuss it with classmates.

Author: .... Length: ....

Publication: .... Publication date: ....

What's the main idea?

How many sources were quoted?

Were there any illustrations? What kind?

What did you learn from this article?

What was the most interesting part for you? Why?

Which do you like better, the way friendships were before social networks or the way things are now? Why?

Write five new vocabulary words, idioms, or expressions related to the article.

  1.
  2.
  3.
  4.
  5.

How would you rate the article on a scale of 1–5, with five being the highest? Why?

> **"Have friends. It's a second existence."**
> —*Baltasar Gracian (1601–1658), Spanish philosopher*

[REPRODUCIBLE]

SEARCH and SHARE

What a Great Game!

Student Name: .... Date: ....

Class: .... Teacher: ....

Think of a great sports match now. Search for a video or article on the Internet (in English) about an exciting game, championship series, or rivalry. Collect information so you can tell your classmates about the exciting sports event.

Here are two websites that might be worthwhile for you to visit: **http://espn.go.com** and **http://sportsillustrated.cnn.com**. Use this worksheet to take notes.

Title: .... Length: ....

Publication: .... Publication date: ....

What event did you choose? Why?

What is the background to this great game?

Can you describe the two rivals?

What happened in the game?

What was your favorite part of the game? Why?

Write three new vocabulary words, idioms, or expressions related to the video or article.

     1.

     2.

     3.

How would you rate the game/match on a scale of 1–5, with five being the highest? Why?

Why did you choose this video or article?

> **"Becoming number one is easier than remaining number one."**
> —*Bill Bradley (1943–), U.S. Senator; American hall of fame basketball player*

[REPRODUCIBLE]

SEARCH and SHARE

TV or not TV (Is that a question?)

Student Name: .... Date: ....

Class: .... Teacher: ....

Search the Internet for a video (in English), taken from a **current television show**. Here are two websites, which might be useful to visit:

http://www.hulu.com and **http://www.imdb.com/sections/tv**

Choose a video segment (*it's not necessary to watch more than ten minutes*), watch it two times, and be prepared to discuss it with classmates.

TV series: .... Type of Show: ....

Title of episode: .... Length: ....

Broadcast network or channel: .... Original airdate: ....

What's the show about?

Can you describe one or two of the main characters?

Did you enjoy the story? Why or why not?

What was the most interesting part for you? Why?

Write five new vocabulary words, idioms, or expressions from the TV show.

1.
2.
3.
4.
5.

How would you rate the video/TV show on a scale of 1–5, with five being the highest? Why?

Why did you choose this video?

> **"In the age of television, image becomes more important than substance."**
> —*S.I. Hayakawa (1906–1992), U.S. senator and linguist*

[REPRODUCIBLE]

SEARCH and SHARE

Exploring New Holidays

Student Name: .... Date: ....

Class: .... Teacher: ....

Search on the Internet for an article (in English) about a favorite holiday or celebration. Choose a holiday that you do <u>not</u> currently celebrate, but that you would like to know more about. Find an article, read it, print it out, and be prepared to discuss it with classmates.

Title: ....

Author: .... Length: ....

Publication: .... Publication date: ....

What is the name of the holiday or celebration you have chosen?

What are two or three important facts about the holiday or celebration?

Are there any opinions in the article? What are they? Whose are they? Do you agree or disagree?

What would you add to the holiday or celebration to make it even better?

What was the most interesting part for you? Why?

Write five new vocabulary words, idioms, or expressions from the article.

1.
2.
3.
4.
5.

How would you rate the article, on a scale of 1–5, with five being the highest? Why?

Why did you choose this article?

> **"Thanksgiving Day is the one day that is truly American."**
> —*O. Henry (1862–1910), American short story writer*

[REPRODUCIBLE]

SEARCH and SHARE

I Like Your Style!

Student Name: .... Date: ....

Class: .... Teacher: ....

Search the web for an article (in English) about a current trend in clothing or fashion. Find an article, read it, print it out, and be prepared to discuss it with classmates.

Title: ....

Author: .... Length: ....

Publication: .... Publication date: ....

Which clothing or fashion trend is described in your article?

How many sources were quoted?

Were there any illustrations? What kind?

What did you learn from this article?

What was the most interesting part for you? Why?

Write five new vocabulary words, idioms, or expressions from the article.

    1.

    2.

    3.

    4.

    5.

How would you rate the article, on a scale of 1–5, with five being the highest? Why?

Why did you choose this article?

> **"Fashion is about exploring different selves."**
> —*Jane Fonda (1937–), actress and former fashion model*

[REPRODUCIBLE]

SEARCH and SHARE

Reducing Stress and Increasing Happiness

Student Name: .... Date: ....

Class: .... Teacher: ....

We live in stressful times. How can we reduce our stress? How can we increase our happiness? Take the five-minute online quiz called "True Happiness Compass" at:

http://apps.bluezones.com/happiness

Answer the questions, read your evaluation, and be prepared to discuss stress management tips with your classmates.

What did you think of the quiz?

How many questions were asked?

Can you recall two of the questions from the quiz?

1.
2.

How would you rate the online quiz, on a scale of 1–5, with five being the highest? Why?

Next, find a recent article about how to cope with stress and increase happiness.

Title: ....

Author: .... Length: ....

Publication: .... Publication date: ....

What's the main idea?

How many sources were quoted?

How reliable were the sources quoted? Why?

How could the article be improved? Why?

How would you rate the article on a scale of 1–5, with five being the highest? Why?

> **"For fast-acting relief, try slowing down."**
> *Lily Tomlin (1939–), American actress*

[REPRODUCIBLE]

SEARCH and SHARE

Finding Advice on Job Interview Techniques

Student Name: .... Date: ....

Class: .... Teacher: ....

Please find a video clip (in English) that you would like to share with your classmates from **YouTube.com, hulu.com,** or **Monster.com** that helps people successfully interview for jobs. Watch the video, take notes, and review it for your classmates.

Video title: ....

Web address: ....

Length: .... Creator: ....

Describe the video.

What interview tips did the video provide?

How practical was the advice? Why?

What do you think was the strongest part? Why?

What was the weakest part? Why?

Who do you think is the target audience for this video?

Why did you choose this video?

How would you rate this video on a scale of 1–5, with five being the highest? Why?

> **"Hiring is a manager's most important job."**
> *Peter F. Drucker (1909–2005), American maagement consultant and author*

[REPRODUCIBLE]

SEARCH and SHARE

Building a Better Budget

Student Name: .... Date: ....

Class: .... Teacher: ....

Where would you like to live in the United States? What would it cost to live your American dream in California, the "Golden State"? The cost of living often depends on location so you need to consider many things when creating a realistic budget.

The California Career Resource Network has created an interactive website called **www.CaliforniaRealityCheck.com** to help estimate budgets. Check it out.

Were you able to successfully complete the budget process? If not, why not?

Did you find any surprises? What?

Where does most of your money go?

Where would you like to spend more? Why?

Where would you like to spend less? Why?

What's your second choice for a possible home in California?

Can you compare the two locations? How are the costs similar? Different?

How would you rate the website on a scale of 1–5, with five being the highest?

Why did you give it that rating?

What do you think are some advantages to living in California? Why?

> **"California is America – only more so."**
> —*Wallace E. Stegner (1909-1993) American historian*

[REPRODUCIBLE]

SEARCH and SHARE

Explore a New American City!

Student Name: .... Date: ....

Class: .... Teacher: ....

Let's go explore a new city. Select one of the ten cities that you would like to visit. Now go find an article – in English – about the American city that you selected and have not yet visited. Read the article and answer the questions below. Be ready to share your research about an American city with your classmates. Your teacher may ask for volunteers to speak in front of the class.

Title: ....

Author: .... Length: ....

Publication: .... Publication date: ....

What's the main idea?

How many sources were quoted?

Were there any illustrations? What kind?

What did you learn from this article?

What was the most interesting part for you? Why?

Write five new vocabulary words, idioms, or expressions related to the article.
   1.
   2.
   3.
   4.
   5.

How would you rate the article on a scale of 1–5, with five being the highest? Why?

Why did you choose this article?

> **"A great city is that which has the greatest men and women."**
> —*Walt Whitman (1819-1892), American poet*

COMPELLING CONVERSATIONS – JAPAN

REPRODUCIBLE SEARCH AND SHARE COLLECTION

Written and Edited by
Eric H. Roth

Shiggy Ichinomiya

Brent Warner

[REPRODUCIBLE]

SEARCH and SHARE

Reviewing Pronunciation Tips on the Internet

_____ / 10

Student Name: .... Date: ....

Class: .... Teacher: ....

Find an article or video on the Internet that describes a typical English-speaking family and their daily life. Watch the video, take notes, and review it for your classmates.

Video title: ....

Web address: ....

Length: .... Creator: ....

1. Describe the video.

2. What pronunciation tips did the video give?

3. Which words or sounds did the video focus on?

4. How practical did you find the advice? Why?

5. What was the strongest part? Why?

6. What was the weakest part? Why?

7. Who do you think is the target audience for this video? Why?

8. Why did you choose this video?

9. How would you rate this video on a scale of 1–5, with 5 being the highest? Why?

> **"I was the kind nobody thought could make it. I had a funny Boston accent. I couldn't pronounce my R's. I wasn't a beauty."**
> —*Barbara Walters (1929–), American television journalist*

[REPRODUCIBLE]

SEARCH and SHARE

Interviewing English Speakers and Tourists

Student Name: .... Date: ....

Class: .... Teacher: ....

Go to a local tourist site, find someone on campus, or meet a neighbor in your neighborhood. Choose a few questions to interview English speakers. Many native English speakers will be happy to help you practice your English conversation skills and share their experiences for a few minutes.

1. Can I ask you a few short questions for my English class?

2. Where are you from?

3. Why did you come to ....?

4. How much time have you spent in .... so far?

5. What do you like most about being in ....?

6. What have you seen so far in ....?

7. What traditional dishes have you eaten so far?

8. Have you found any bargains shopping yet? What?

9. How do you travel from one place to another? Do you walk? Take a bus? Other?

10. What are you planning on doing tomorrow?

11. Will you be going to ....?

12. Do you expect to go to ....?

13. What are some other places you would like to see in ....? Why?

14. How would you describe your time in .... so far? Why?

15. Would you recommend visiting .... to your family and friends?

Remember to thank your conversation partner for their time and wish them a good day.

> **"Tourists don't know where they've been; travelers don't know where they're going."**
> —*Paul Theroux (1941–), American writer and novelist*

[REPRODUCIBLE]

SEARCH and SHARE

My Dream Home Worksheet

_____ / 10

Student Name: .... Date: ....

Class: .... Teacher: ....

Have you ever thought about living in a dream home? Use your imagination, knowledge, and research to describe the dream home where you would like to live. Use the vocabulary learned in this lesson. Imagine the possibilities. Dream big!

1. Location:

2. Who will live in your dream home?

3. What does the outside look like?

4. How many rooms are there?

5. Describe your bedroom.

6. Describe the room where your family gathers.

7. Describe another room.

8. How would you describe the furniture in your dream home?

9. What else makes this home special?

10. What other information or details can you share?

Be prepared to share your dream with your classmates in class! Show your knowledge and research to describe your dream home.

> **"There is a role and function for beauty in our time."**
> —*Tadao Ando (1941–), Japanese architect*

[REPRODUCIBLE]

SEARCH and SHARE
Choosing a Local Restaurant

```
_____ / 10
```

Student Name: .... Date: ....

Class: .... Teacher: ....

Can you recommend a good place for dinner around here? Find and share a positive review for a local restaurant that you like. Pick a favorite local restaurant, do some research, and pick the best review—in Japanese or in English. Use this worksheet to tell us about the review. Remember restaurant reviews should provide examples and details. Tell us about a special restaurant—in English—and help us find a place to eat delicious food.

Restaurant: .... Location: ....

Review: .... Reviewer: ....

1. Why did you pick this review?

2. How does the reviewer describe the restaurant? What kind of food does it serve?

3. When was the review written?

4. What do you know about the reviewer?

5. What does the reviewer say about the restaurant's atmosphere?

6. How did the reviewer describe the restaurant's service?

7. What did the reviewer eat?

8. What was the best part of the restaurant review?

9. Does the reviewer recommend the restaurant? Why?

10. How often have you been to the restaurant? What makes this restaurant special?

> **"One man's meat is another man's poison."**
> —*Latin proverb*

[REPRODUCIBLE]

SEARCH and SHARE

How Do You Spend Your Time?

_____ / 10

Student Name: .... Date: ....

Class: .... Teacher: ....

Enter the amount of time you spend on each of the following activities on a typical weekday. Use your best estimate or guess for each category.

	hours / minutes
sleeping	_____ : _____
eating and drinking	_____ : _____
housework/cleaning up	_____ : _____
attending classes	_____ : _____
working at a job	_____ : _____
commuting/driving	_____ : _____
playing sports and exercising	_____ : _____
using your cell phone	_____ : _____
watching TV	_____ : _____
attending religious services/praying	_____ : _____
socializing and relaxing	_____ : _____

For any of the above activities, would you say that you spend more or less time on it compared to other students in your class?

> **"All the treasures of the earth cannot bring back one lost moment."**
> —*French proverb*

[REPRODUCIBLE]

SEARCH and SHARE

Always Be Yourself

Student Name: .... Date: ....

Class: .... Teacher: ....

For better or for worse, many Americans often pride themselves on their individualism. The mass media often reinforce this idea in entertainment and school. Find a video about being yourself on YouTube.com or another video sharing site.

1. What is the video or series segment about?

2. Can you describe one or two of the people or characters?

3. Did the main person or character face a problem? What was it?

4. What was the main idea of the video?

5. What was the most interesting part for you? Why?

6. Write five new vocabulary words, idioms, or expressions related to the topic.

   a.
   b.
   c.
   d.
   e.

7. Do you think "being yourself" is always a good idea? Why? Why not?

8. How would you rate the video on a scale of 1–5, with 5 being the highest? Why?

> **"Be yourself. Everyone else is already taken."**
> —*Oscar Wilde (1856–1900), Irish playwright*

[REPRODUCIBLE]

SEARCH and SHARE

	_____ / 10

Watching Our World Change

Student Name: .... Date: ....

Class: .... Teacher: ....

Have you heard about TED (Technology, Entertainment, Design) Talks yet? These can be fascinating, surprising, and sometimes controversial talks by global experts in many disciplines. The presenters give highly personal presentations that address many important and interesting topics in short, engaging talks. The exceptional pace of change—technological, social, and economic—remains a constant TED theme.

Give yourself time to explore TED.com, browsing by topic or speaker. Find a short video on a topic of particular interest to you that you can recommend. Watch it twice or more, answer the following questions, and be prepared to share your recommendation. You can also read the subtitles if that will help you better understand the presentation.

Title: .... Location: ....

Speaker: .... Date: ....

1. Why did you choose this TED talk?

2. How did the presentation begin?

3. What is the theme of the talk?

4. What did you learn from this TED talk?

5. What did the speaker want to accomplish?

6. What do you believe is the best thing about this TED talk? Why?

7. How did the speaker connect to his audience? (humor, visual aids, etc.)

8. Did the speaker convince you? Why?

9. How would you rate this TED talk on a scale of 1–5, with 5 being the highest?

10. Why are you recommending this particular talk to your classmates?

> **"Make change your friend."**
> —_William (Bill) Jefferson Clinton (1946–), 42nd U.S. President_

[REPRODUCIBLE]

SEARCH and SHARE

Give a Product Review

_____ / 10

Student Name: .... Date: ....

Class: .... Teacher: ....

Product reviews are increasingly popular, and you can find many places to share reviews. For your next class, pick a consumer product to review. Do some research online about the product. Find at least two sources of information. Then fill in this worksheet, and create a product review to share with your classmates.

Product: .... Company: ....

Sources: .... Date: ....

1. Do you own the product?

2. What is the purpose of the product?

3. Who is the target audience for this product? Who usually uses it?

4. How is the product used?

5. What does the product cost?

6. What competitors does the product have?

7. What are some disadvantages of the product?

8. Are there some possible dangers or misuses of the product?

9. What did you learn during your research about this product?

10. Do you recommend this product for your classmates? Why?

11. How do you rate the product on a scale of 1–5, with 5 being the highest? Why?

> **"The customer is always right."**
> —*American proverb*

[REPRODUCIBLE]

SEARCH and SHARE

Documenting Moments in Time

_____ / 10

Student Name: .... Date: ....

Class: .... Teacher: ....

Documentary photographs capture important moments in time. Visit the Library of Congress collection at www.loc.gov/pictures to find a special historical photograph that captures your imagination. Print it out and share it with your classmates.

Title: ....

Photographer: ....

Historical Context: .... Date: ....

1. Describe the photograph. What is going on?

2. How did the photographer compose his picture? Where are your eyes drawn?

3. What historical moment does it capture? Does it do it well?

4. Why do you think the photographer chose to take this picture?

5. Why did you choose this photograph?

6. What did you learn from it?

7. Do you think a photograph like this would still be taken today? Why? Why not?

8. On a scale of 1–5, with 5 being the highest, how would you rate the photograph? Why?

> **"There are always two people in every picture: the photographer and the viewer."**
> —Ansel Adams (1902–1984), American photographer and environmentalist

[REPRODUCIBLE]

SEARCH and SHARE

Be a Movie Critic!

_____ / 10

Student Name: .... Date: ....

Class: .... Teacher: ....

Can you recommend an excellent movie? Select one of your favorite movies, go to the website www.imdb.com, and research the selected film. Take notes. A strong movie review will combine both facts and opinions. Use this short worksheet to describe the movie and prepare to share your informed opinion with your classmates.

Title: .... Genre: ....

Director: .... Date: .... Length: ....

Actors/Actresses: ....

Awards? ....

How many times have you watched the movie? .... Where? ....

PLOT INFORMATION:

1. Where does the movie take place?

2. When does the movie take place?

3. Who are the main characters? Can you briefly describe them?

4. What happens in the movie?

5. What makes the movie interesting?

6. What is the best part? Why?

7. Does the movie surprise the audience? How? How could it be a better film?

8. How did you feel when the movie ended? Why?

9. Is there anything else you want to tell me about your favorite movie?

10. Who do you think would like this movie? Why?

11. Would you give a thumbs up (positive) or thumbs down (negative) review?

12. On a scale of 1–5 stars, with 5 being the highest, how do you rate this movie? Why?

"Every great film should seem new every time you see it."
—_Roger Ebert (1942–2013), American film critic_

[REPRODUCIBLE]

SEARCH and SHARE

Exploring a Foreign City!

Student Name: .... Date: ....

Class: .... Teacher: ....

Let's explore a foreign city together! Find an article in English about a city outside of Japan. Carefully read the article and summarize it, then bring the article to class and share some information with your classmates.

Title: ....

Author: .... Publication date: ....

Length: .... Publication: ....

1. What's the main idea?

2. How many sources were quoted?

3. Were there any illustrations? What kind?

4. What did you learn about the country where this city is located?

5. What was the most interesting part for you? Why?

6. Write down five new vocabulary words, idioms, or expressions.

    1.

    2.

    3.

    4.

    5.

7. How would you rate the article on a scale of 1–5, with 5 being the highest? Why?

8. Why did you choose this article?

"The bold adventurer succeeds the best."

—*Ovid (43 B.C.E.–17 C.E.) Roman poet*

About the Authors

Eric H. Roth

Eric H. Roth teaches international graduate students the pleasures and perils of academic writing and public speaking in English at the University of Southern California (USC). He also consults English language schools on communicative methods to effectively teach English.

Given a full scholarship as a Lilly Scholar, Roth studied philosophy and American history at Wabash College (1980-1984), and received his M.A. in Media Studies from the New School (1988). Since 1992, Roth has taught English to high school, community college, adult, and university students. Highlights of his career include: teaching the first Saturday morning citizenship class in Santa Monica (1994); directing the CES Adult Education Center (1995-1998); working with international students in summer IEP programs at UCLA Extension (1997-2000, 2003-2005); teaching USC engineering students in Madrid, Spain (2007) and Paris, France (2008); and directing the APU International High School in Ho Chi Minh City, Vietnam (2009).

Roth co-authored Compelling Conversations: Questions and Quotations on Timeless Topics in 2006 to help English language learners increase their English fluency. Recommended by English Teaching Professional magazine, the advanced ESL textbook has been used in over 50 countries in English classrooms and conversation clubs. Easy English Times, an adult literacy newspaper, has published a monthly column, "Instant Conversation Activities," based on the book since 2008. The first specific version for a particular country, Vietnam, was published in 2011. Future versions for Japan, Korea, Israel, Mexico, and Romania are anticipated.

A member of the USC faculty since 2003, Roth is a member of numerous professional organizations including: California Association of Teaching English to Speakers of Other Languages (CATESOL); the International Communication Association (ICA); the International Professors Project (IPP); and Teaching English to Speakers of Other Languages (TESOL). Roth, a master lecturer, has given several CATESOL conference presentations and led many teacher training workshops. The USC Center for Scholarly Technology awarded Roth two teaching with technology grants in 2011. He has given several CATESOL and TESOL conference presentations and shares his teaching experiences on the blog, **www.CompellingConversations.com/blog.**

Mark Treston

Mark Treston has over fifteen years of teaching and management experience, and specializes in world history and teaching English. He is also the author of "Gailee" and "North Korean Memoirs," both outstanding historical novels based on real events, and a co-author of the forthcoming *Compelling American Conversations: Teacher Guide* as well as the *Reproducible Guide*. Mark is currently working on *Creating a Quality English Language School: Insights from the Classrooms, Owners, and Regulators* for Chimayo Press. The publication date will be announced later this year.

Mark taught throughout the world as well as domestically. Mark cofounded two colleges and assisted countless others through the complicated world of compliance. Mark serves as a consultant for publishing firms and higher education institutes. Mark speaks several languages and enjoys travelling as much as he likes writing about his travels. Mark also serves on the board of two colleges and volunteers as an educational consultant for non-profit learning centers. Mark lives in Los Angeles with his wife and two boys.

Robert Glynn

Robert is atenured teacher in the Los Angeles School District, where he wrote the Citizenship Preparation Workbook and several episodes of Putting English to Work 1, a video series which was subsequently chosen by the United States Department of Homeland Security/ICE as the nation's official course for learners of English as a Second Language. He has also taught in the Santa Monica-Malibu Unified School District, working with the former Director of ESL for the United States Department of Education.

Chimayo Press is an independent educational publishing company committed to publishing niche books that create compelling conversations, deepen relationships and celebrate the human spirit. We launched in 2005 with one advanced level English as a Second Language (ESL) title – Compelling Conversations: Questions and Quotations on Timeless Topics – from authors Eric H. Roth and Toni Aberson. This fluency-focused textbook has blossomed into series meeting the varying needs of English language learners and their teachers in over 50 countries.

Chimayo Press is named for our amazingly communicative, talented and loving first border collie. We met him soon after a visit to the inspirational New Mexico town. That's Chimayo's image in our logo.

Praise For Compelling American Conversations

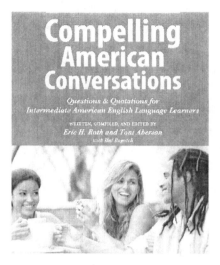

"How can so much learning be in just one book? Compelling American Conversations is all that an ESL teacher or student needs to use in their course. With clear, easy to follow directions, students learn necessary details about American English and culture, practice critical thinking, expand vocabulary and idioms, as they converse in real, natural adult English. Included in the "Search and Share" component are marvelous lessons on using the Internet. An extra bonus is that any of the conversations, quotes, etc. can be used as writing prompts. The book is fun and stimulating and, fortunately, very accessible for the inter-mediate learner."

—Planaria Price
Author, *Life in the USA* and *Realistically Speaking*

"Conversational English proficiency can only be acquired by engaging in authentic English conversations. The academic approach used all too frequently in conventional ESL classrooms consistently fails at helping English learners become fluent English speakers. Compelling American Conversations fills the gap left by inadequate curricula by offering engaging topics and prompts that become the starting point for thoughtful and meaningful conversations. I highly recommend it."

—Nathan D. Crandall, M.A.
Founder, The Fluency Coach: **www.thefluencycoach.com**

"Compelling American Conversations is a great textbook for teaching conversational American English to ESL learners. It teaches the students topic by topic how to start a conversation with small talk leading up to a more serious discussion using relevant vocabulary and global idioms within the context of American culture. It also focuses on teaching the students how to ask questions as well as answering them. This is something that they will all need in the real world. I highly recommend it as either a main textbook or as supplementary material for any ESL instructor to use with intermediate to advanced level students who want to improve their oral skills."

—Eva Owen
EFL/ESL Instructor

"Finally, a book that is designed for our needs. As the director of a film school, one of our biggest obstacles for the international students is to bridge the gap between spoken English and our students' background in ESL. Our international students find the English spoken by native studio personnel, actors, directors etc. All of these students have already scored high enough on their TOEFL yet they still lack communicative skills to interact with Americans in the "biz." For these reason we implemented a crash course for all incoming international students using Compelling American Conversations. We have already seen the results in terms of the general ability of the students to communicate more effectively with Americans on the set. More importantly, the students feel more confident now when directing a film, auditioning for actors and actresses or scouting for location. Bottom line is that the book is practical and meant for students that are trying to enhance their communicative skills."

—Chisako Yokoyama
director of the International School of Motion Pictures

Compelling Conversations

Other titles in this series:

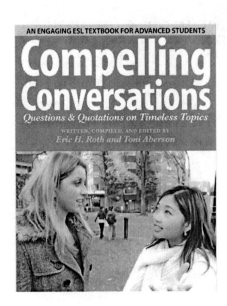

CPSIA information can be obtained at www.ICGtesting.com
Printed in the USA
LVOW09s1927101115

461901LV00012B/272/P

9 781512 226751